Colorado

Colorado

1982 Published by Colourpicture Publishers, Inc.
76 Atherton St.
Boston, MA 02130

ISBN 0-938440-09-8

Edited by Penelope P. Massey

PHOTO CREDITS:

Dwayne Easterling	Russell Ohlson
J. F. Ogsbury	Ed Cooper
Bob Petley	Glen Wood
Larry Sebring	Henry Lansford
Marian Blank	Dick Dickson
Bob McMillan	Tony Schweikle
Ted and Lois Matthews	Jack Watkin
Charles S. Motisher, Jr.	Steve Pierce
Lew Dakan	Peter Runyon
James Blank	Roach Photos
Don Ceppi	Herman Birlauf
Geo. R. Dickson	Mel Schieltz

Distributed by: G. R. Dickson Co., 932 Inca St., Denver, CO 80204
Flatiron Postcard Co., P.O. Box 961, Boulder, CO 80306
Petley Studios, Inc., 4051 E. Van Buren, Phoenix, AZ 85008

Overleaf: Long's Peak and Glacier Gorge from Bear Lake in Rocky Mountain National Park.

CONTENTS

Colorado • Above All 7

Colorado's Earliest Inhabitants 17

Indian and Spanish Heritages 21

There's Gold in Them Thar Hills 25

National Parks and Monuments 29

Things to See and Do 57

Mile High City 67

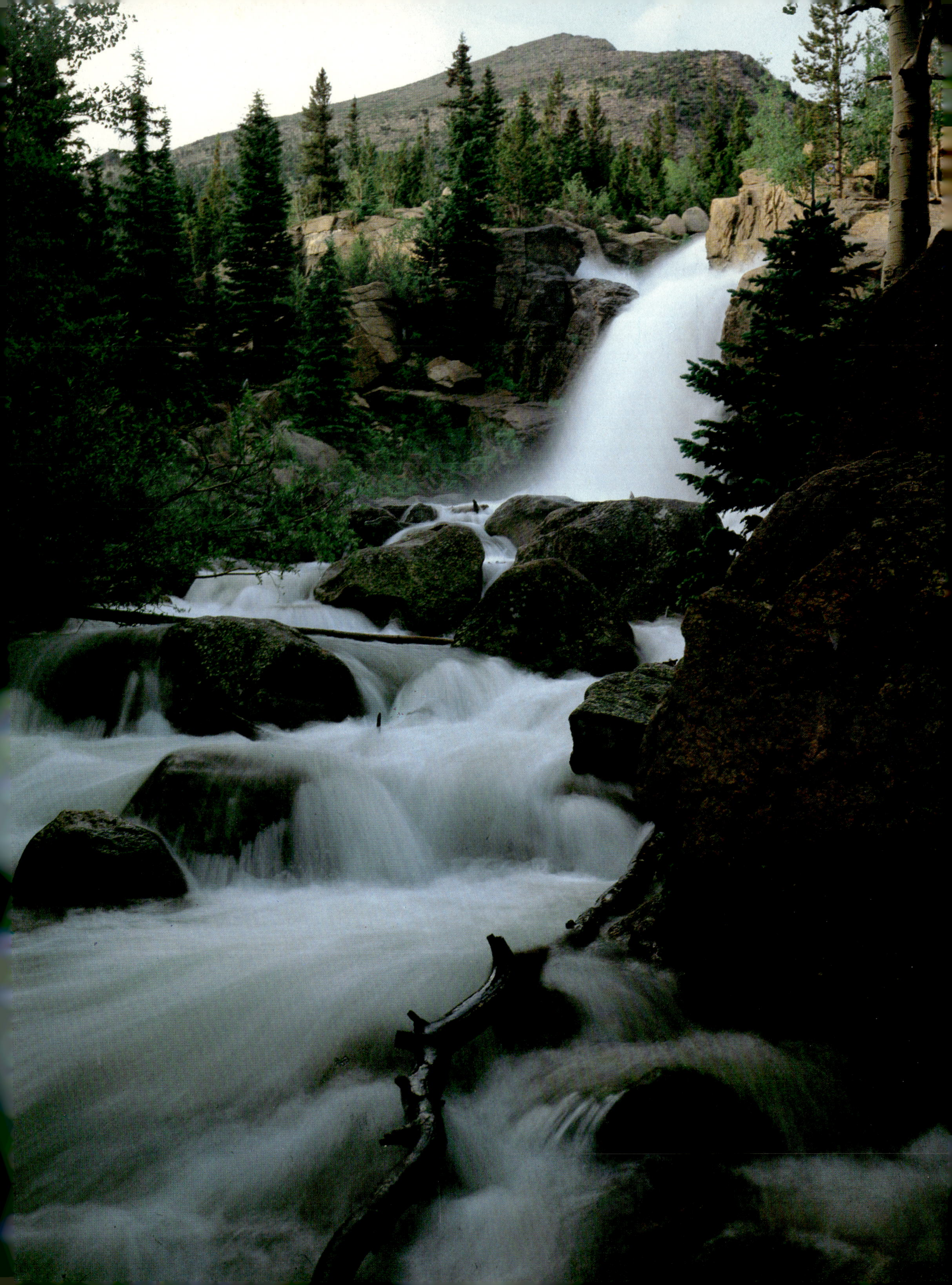

COLORADO · ABOVE ALL

"Across the central third of North America, for more than 1,000 miles, the prairie rolls westward, shifting from the moisture of the Mississippi River Valley to the aridity of the high plains. And then, with swiftness and drama, the levelness ends. Looming before him, the traveler sees the great face of the American Rockies, the snow-capped spine of a continent. The Midwest has ended, the mountains have begun."
Neal R. Peirce

This is Colorado...the state which holds a mountain area more than six times that of Switzerland, with fifty-three snow-crested peaks towering more than 14,000 feet above sea level, and a total of 1,143 mountains which rise to an altitude of 10,000 feet or more.

There's snow. Lots of it. Fluffy-light and powdery-dry...enough to make a skier "giggle". There are National Forests. Eleven of them...with a total of 15 million acres for nearly every variety of outdoor sporting event...hiking, backpacking, boating, fishing, ballooning, rockhounding, jeeping, et al. Another half-million acres are National Parks, Monuments, Recreation Areas, and Grasslands. And there are thirty State Parks and State Recreation Areas.

There's marvelous history. This is where Buffalo Bill, Kit Carson, Molly Brown, Butch Cassidy, Calamity Jane, Bat Masterson, and Soapy Smith (to name a few) made their mark. Legends and local traditions abound. Even today, stories about the gold in "them thar hills" are spun with vivid imagination. A traveler really CAN find cowboys, and take a poke at being one if the desire is there. And anyone with a hankering for prospecting is welcome to stand in a stream with a gold pan...and a lot of patience. The wild by-gone days of unauthorized bank withdrawals are outmoded, of course, but there are plenty of historical buildings, cemeteries, museums, and libraries which awaken those flavorful days.

There's earlier history too. The oldest apartment house in the world (not for rent) is in southwestern Colorado. Built into a cliff face, it is one of numerous existing dwellings which are evidence of the advanced and complex culture of the Anasazi (the ancient ones), whose historical evolution can be traced from about the time of Christ to A.D. 1300.

There's a touch of urban which contributes to a colorful past and a colorful future. Boulder, Colorado Springs, Denver, Fort Collins, Grand Junction, Pueblo, Trinidad, and other cities offer an intriguing blend of attractions, from flamboyant Victorian architecture to space exploration and atomic research. Indeed, Colorado is making as much history today as it did in the mid 1800's. The Martin Marietta Corporation,

Left: The impressive Alberta Falls in the Rocky Mountain National Park is reached via a short walk from the Glacier Gorge Junction on the Bear Lake Road.

Overleaf: Million Dollar Highway

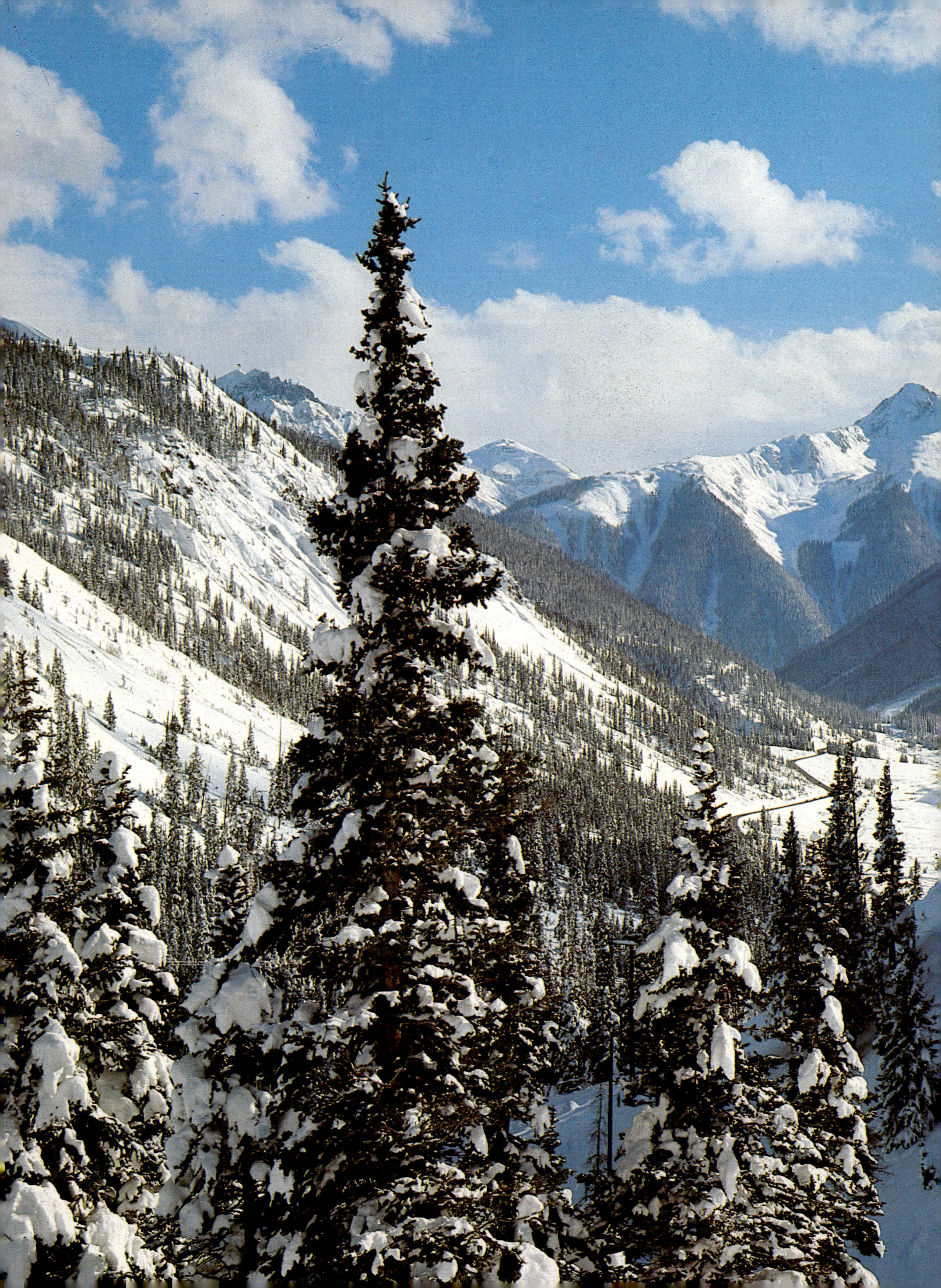

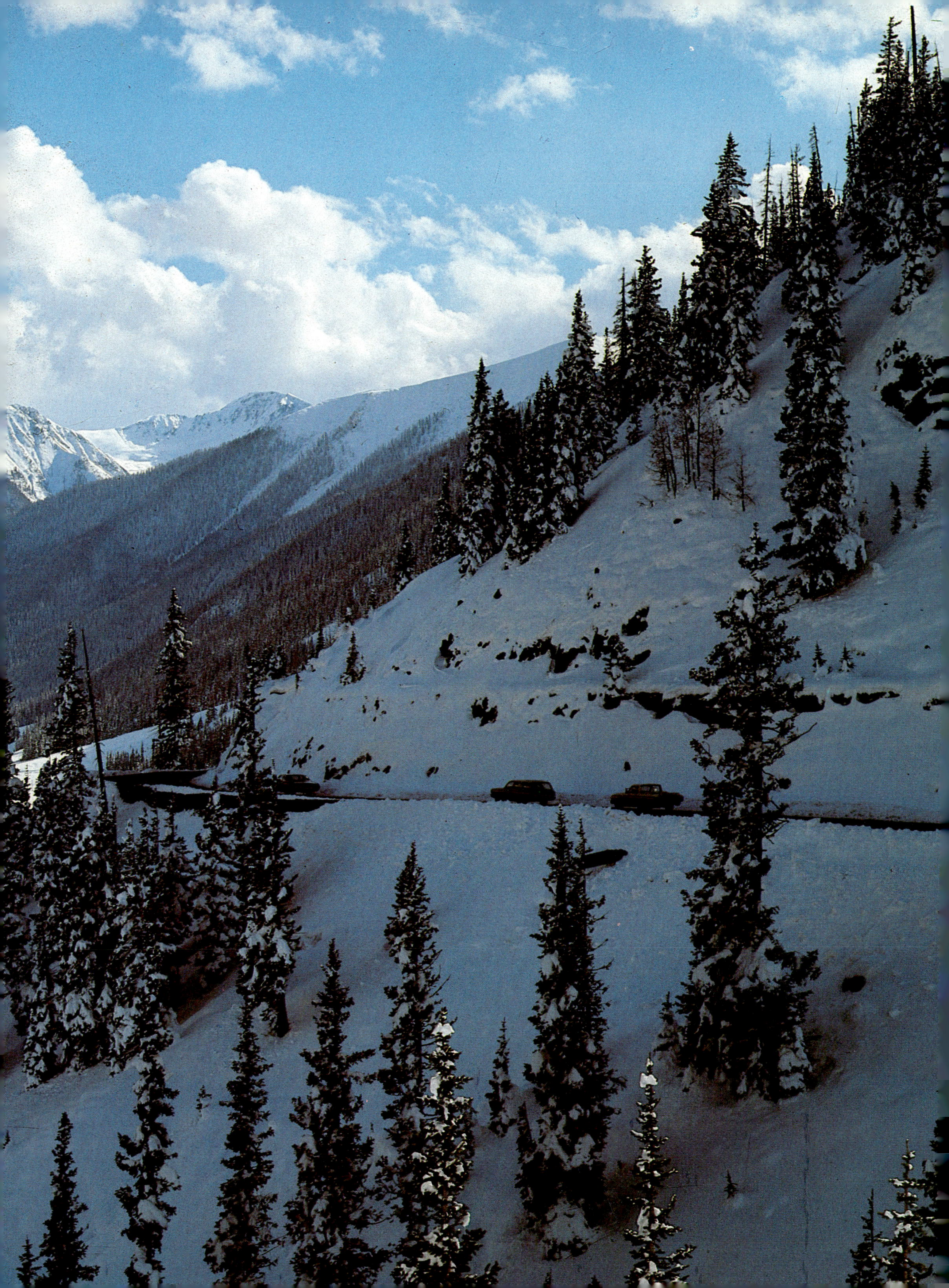

Left: Long's Peak and the Keyboard of the Winds as viewed from the trail to Dream Lake in Rocky Mountain National Park.

Below: Gore Range along Blue River

Right: Red Oaks accentuate a background of snow-covered mountain peaks of the San Juan Mountains in southwestern Colorado.

Overleaf: This sandstone monolith, 536 feet high, in Monument Canyon, is an outstanding scenic and geologic feature in a wonderland of rock.

which produces launch and space vehicles for our space programs, is located just southwest of Denver. Only two decades ago, a major production facility was built by the Atomic Energy Commission between Denver and Boulder on Rocky Flats. Other facilities, including one to help estimate the nation's uranium and thorium deposits have been recently built.

Also, the diverse and natural landscape offers a wealth of mineral deposits. Though gold and silver have gained less importance because of extensive mining, other minerals have been discovered and are substantially influencing Colorado's growth. All those minerals with unpronounceable names such as molybdenum, vanadium, pyrite, beryllium, and columbite-tantalite, are major mineral extractions contributing to Colorado's function in the nation's energy policies. The main energy minerals consist of coal, crude petroleum, natural gas, and oil shale. In fact, the largest oil shale reserves in the world are in northwestern Colorado...just waiting development.

Colorado IS colorful! How well it earned its name from the Spanish. Its history is written in names of mountain ranges and passes, cities, towns, national parks, and monuments. And it continues to make history through sophisticated scientific research and development.

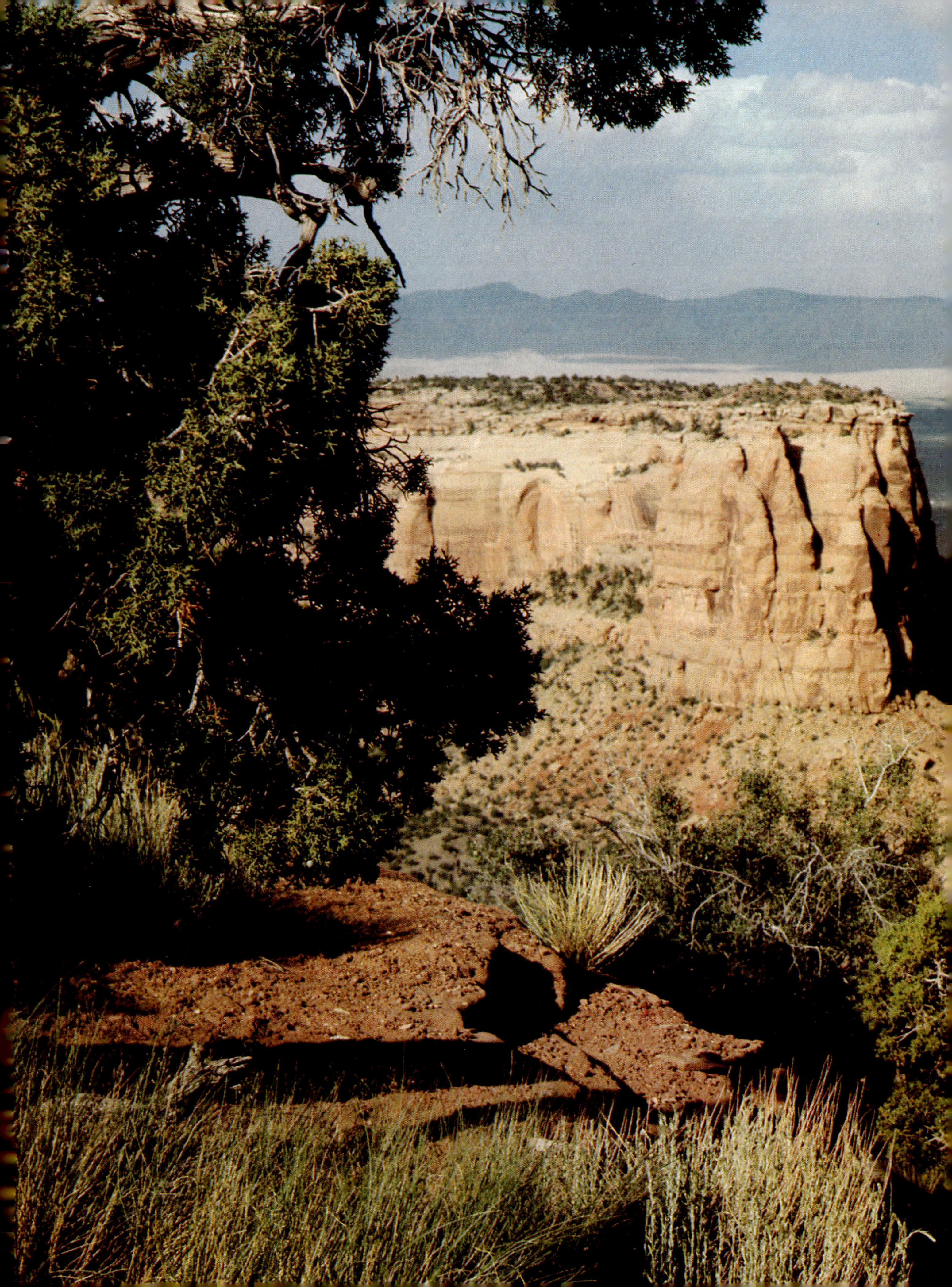

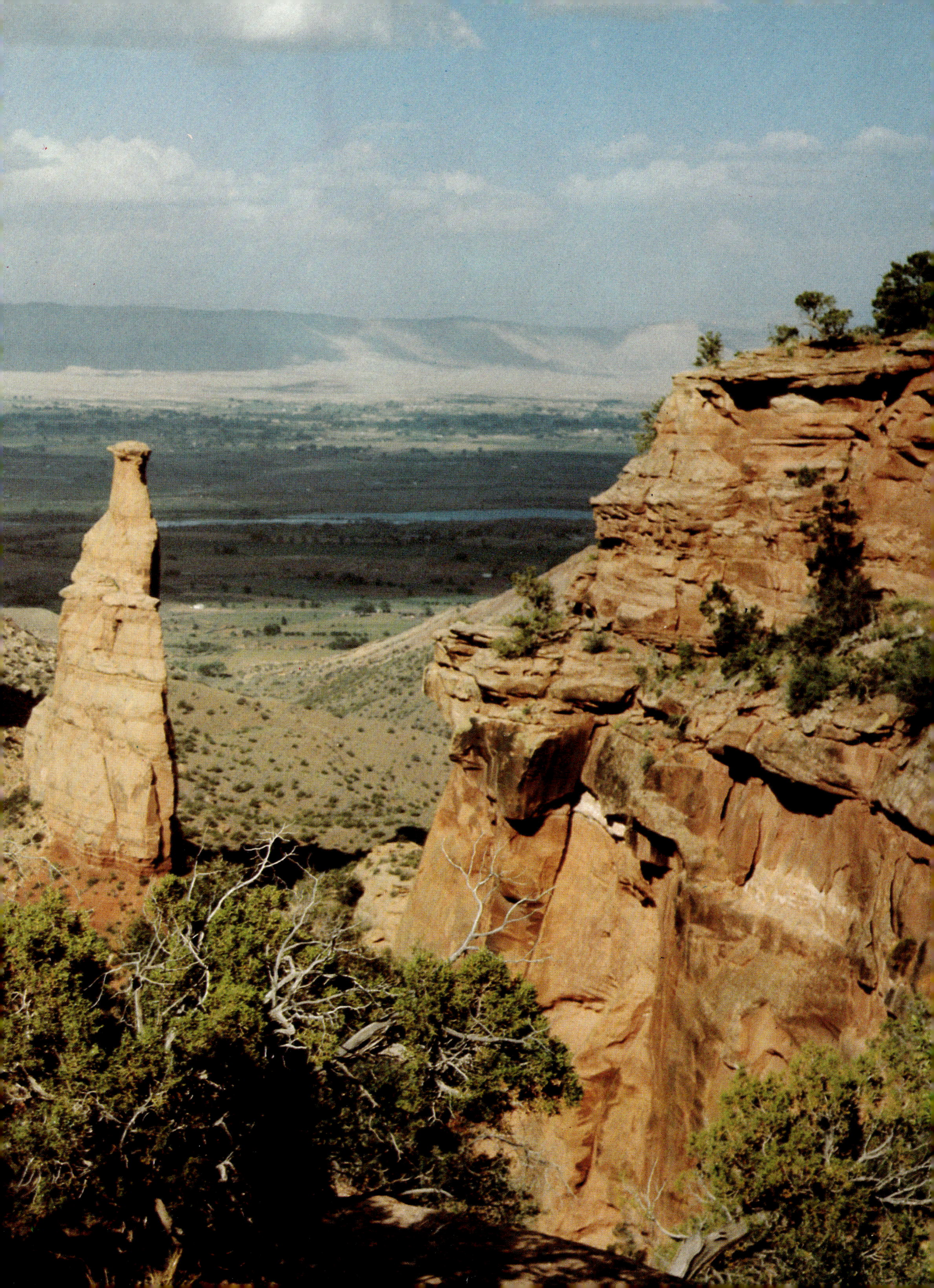

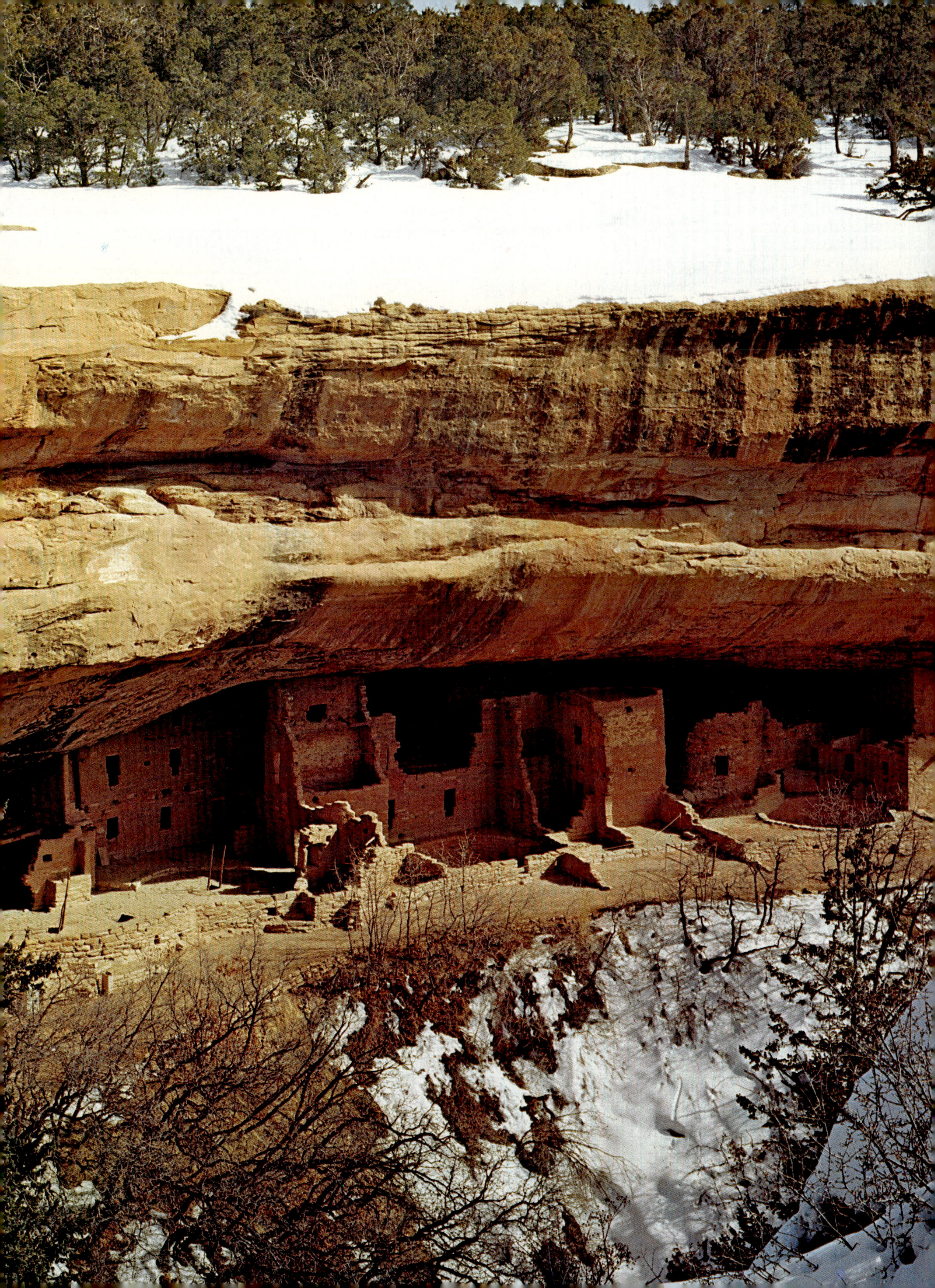

COLORADO'S EARLIEST INHABITANTS

"There is nothing that solidifies and strengthens a nation like reading the nation's history, whether that history is recorded in books, or embodied in customs, institutions, and monuments."
J. Anderson

The story of Colorado's inhabitants really begins some 15,000 to 20,000 thousand years ago when Asiatic men began their migration to the New World. Artifacts which have been found during twentieth century archeological digs have allowed a systematic reconstruction of the life of Colorado's earliest human...the Folsom Man. Preserved fossils reveal the use of arrows and lances for hunting camels, bison, and mammoths which have long been extinct. Over thousands of years, and in different areas, these people developed different traditions and cultures, and created better, more sophisticated weapons and tools. They were constantly on the move, seeking out the herds which provided them with food and clothing.

Some of the richest fossil deposits were excavated near Fort Collins during the 1930's by the Smithsonian Institution. Many artifacts used by Folsom Man were unearthed. Stone beads, lanceheads, scrappers, and blades were found, but there was no trace of skeletal remains, leading some to believe that odd burial traditions may have been part of the Folsom Man's culture. The mystery of their disappearance has never been solved.

Thousands of years went by, and other groups of men began to settle in small villages along river banks and in the plains. These peoples were very primitive Indians, knowing nothing about agriculture. But as their culture progressed, they began to plant and harvest corn, and soon their nomadic lifestyles came to an end.

Far to the south and west of the San Juan Mountains lived a group called Anasazi, meaning "ancient ones". From about the time of Christ to A.D. 1300, these people developed higher skills. The earlier Anasazi became very adept at weaving baskets and containers, and became known as the Basket Makers. Skillfully made baskets actually held water or served as cooking containers in which hot stones were dropped to heat the water. They harvested other crops, such as beans and squash, but considered corn their staple.

By A.D. 700, the Anasazi culture had gone into a period known as the Pueblo, and between A.D. 1050 and 1300, the Pueblo's built complex dwellings on mesa tops and carved large community houses in cliff faces. Centuries old, these great cliff dwellings still stand, preserving some of the most fascinating building achievements by primitive man. Mesa Verde National Park contains the best examples of cliff dwellings and artifacts, the largest and most outstanding of which is Cliff Palace...an apartment complex dug into the cliff's face some 200 feet above the canyon floor and having more than 200 rooms. It was, at one time, the home of some 400 people.

Left: Mesa Verde National Park Spruce Tree House.

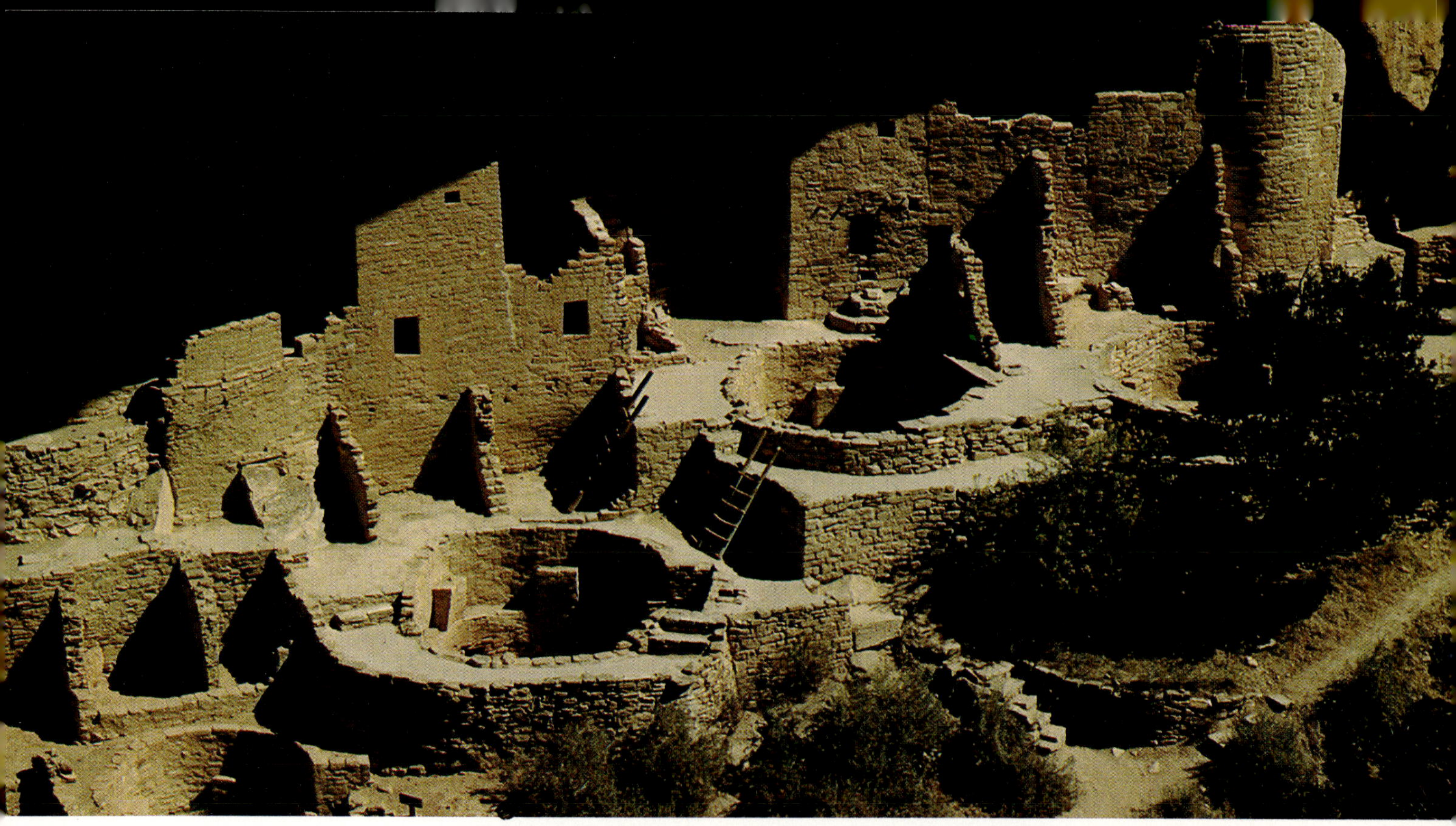
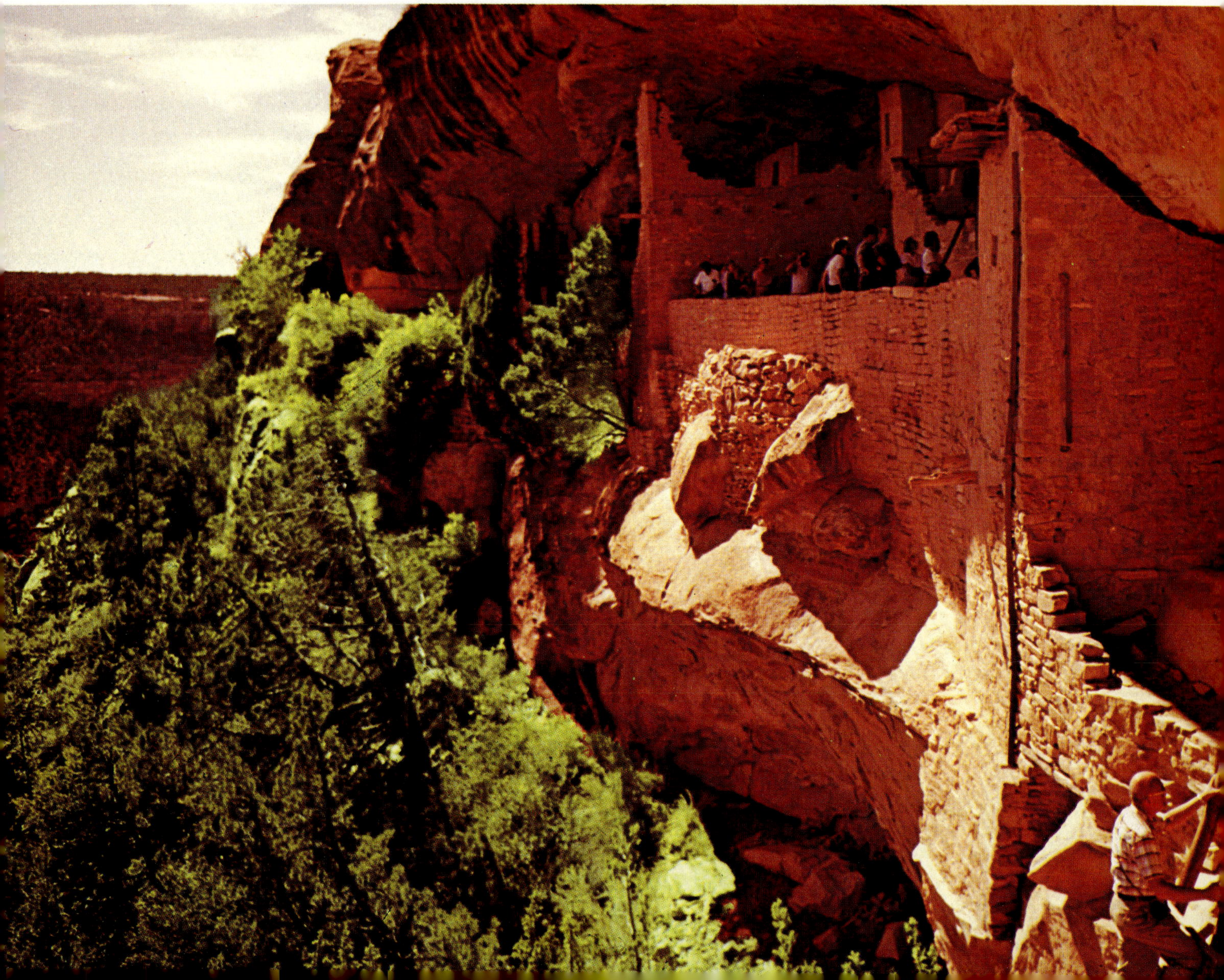

There are also remnants of pithouses—shallow holes in the earth usually roofed with straw or grass—each apparently intended to be shared by a single family. Originally, these pithouses were nothing more than granaries, but converting their use into dwellings gave the Pueblos ample protection from weather and allowed them to live atop the mesas where they could grow and harvest crops. Later, the pithouses were retained for ceremonial purposes and acquired the name KIVA, a term borrowed from the Hopi Indians.

By the beginning of the fourteenth century, the "Pueblo Period" came to an end. Though the cause is speculative...famine, drought, disease, or unfriendly raids...the Pueblos abandoned their villlages in search of a more hospitable environment.

This entire span of time, up until the sixteenth century, is considered prehistoric since no written records were left by these early inhabitants. It wasn't until the arrival of the Spaniards that historical records were kept, at which point began a new era called the "historical period".

Upper left: Detail of Cliff Palace. Note kivas in foreground.

Left: A tourist climbs an Indian Ladder to the Balcony House on the National Park tour through the spectacular Cliff Dwellings built by the ancient Indians.

Overleaf: Reached by new beautiful highways like the Navajo Trail, no trip is complete without the opportunity to explore enormous prehistoric ruins deserted by a people that vanished nearly a thousand years ago. This view is of Cliff Palace, the largest cliff dwelling known.

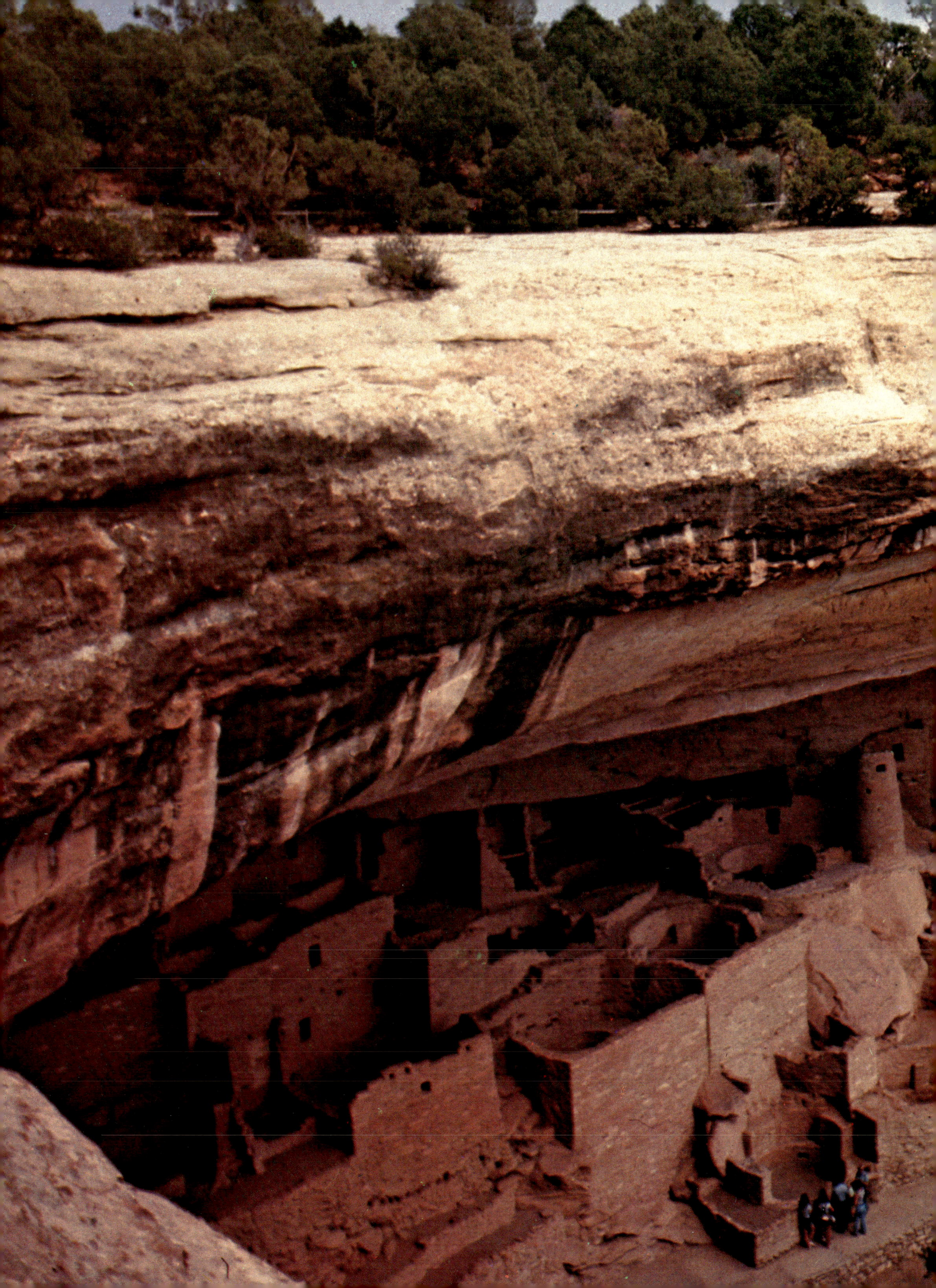

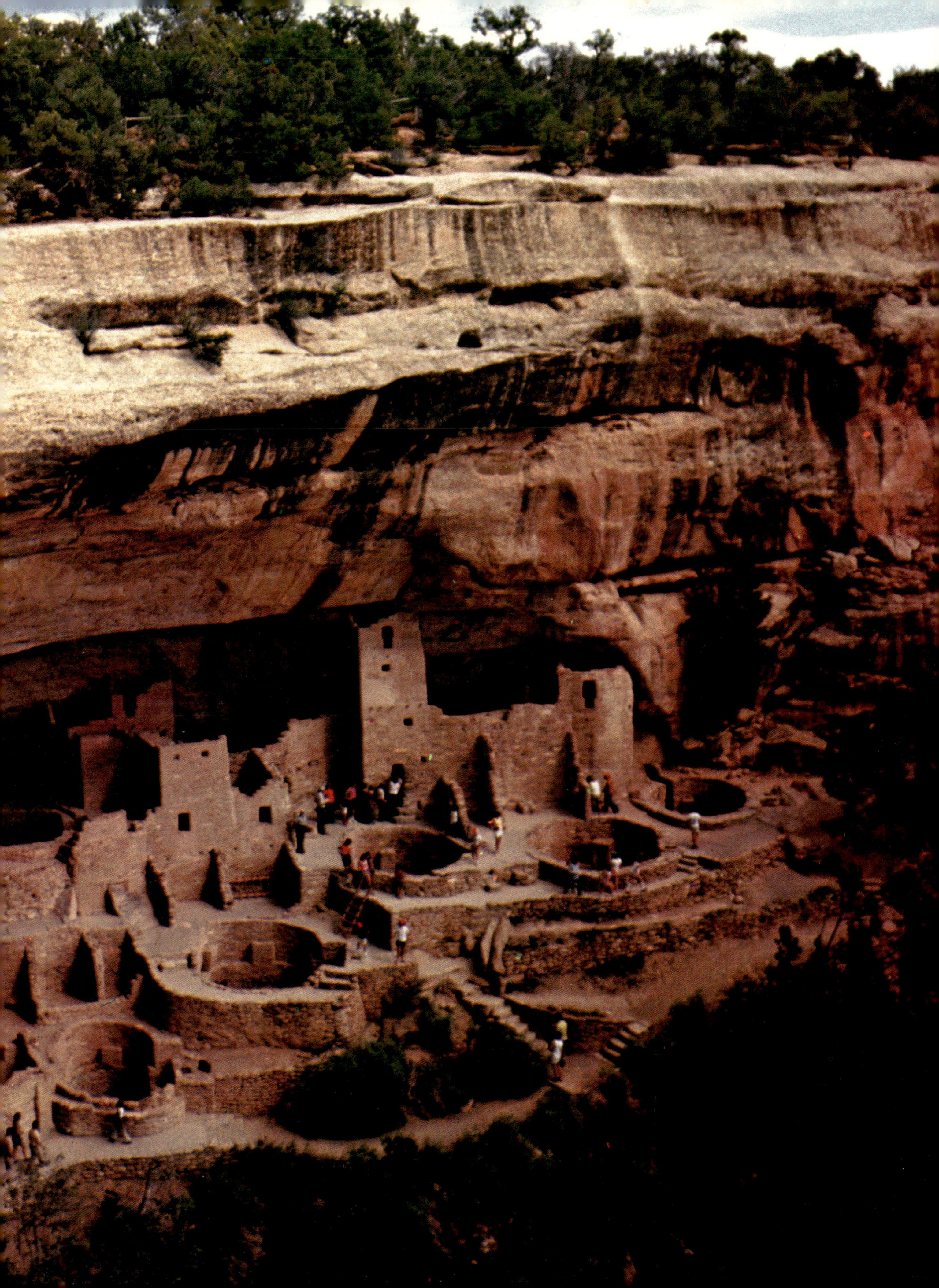

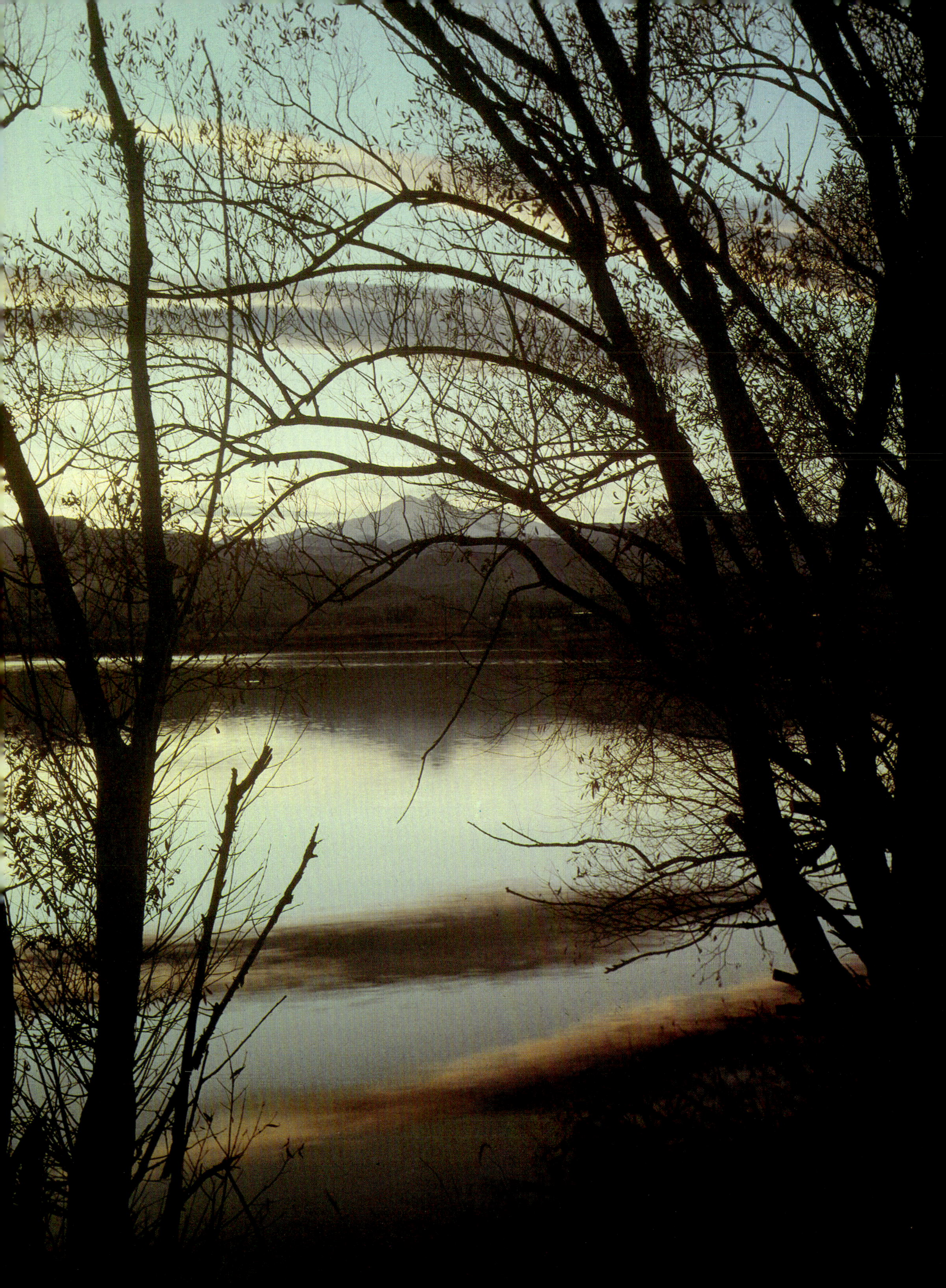

INDIAN AND SPANISH HERITAGES

A Ute tribe camped on the shores of Grand Lake was attacked by Cheyenne and Arapaho tribes. While most of the Ute warriors were killed, the women and children were placed on a raft and pushed out into the lake for their safety. A huge storm capsized the raft, and all were drowned. Mists rising from Grand Lake are believed to be the spirits of the unfortunates.
An Indian Legend

When the first whites began to explore what is now Colorado, they found most of the land was occupied by two major Indian tribes. The Shoshonean roamed the mountains and a small section of the southern plains, while the Algonkian tribes lived throughout the northeastern plains.

The main tribe of the Shoshonean stock were the mountain-dwelling Utes, the only native Colorado Indians. The earliest Utes lived just above the level of subsistence, with meager plant fibers and rabbit furs for clothing, piles of brush for housing, and seeds, berries and a snake or two for food. When the Utes acquired bows from the Navajos, and horses from the Spaniards, their lifestyle changed from misery to ecstasy. They became masters at trading and bartering with the Spaniards, acquiring buckskins, beads, and more horses. They traveled to the plains to hunt buffalo, and make war with the Arapaho and Cheyenne. They tanned deerskin into wonderfully soft hides, built teepees, adorned themselves with feathers, and generally lived in affluence.

Learning to make the most of their environment, they herded their horses from one location to another according to the seasons, taking advantage of the best grasses for grazing and mildest climates for enjoyment. The Utes, perhaps no more than 3,500 of them in total, were not nomads as such, but were very loose-knit bands who knew the streams, mountains, food and water sources, and moved about to their advantage. They did not know enough to group together in defense of their claimed territory.

Ultimately, the miners began to encroach on their homeland, resulting in a frustrated band of Utes massacring eleven people at the White River Agency in 1879. Nathan C. Meeker, an unfortunate Indian Agent, along with ten of his unfortunate employees, were slain by the Utes in an historical uprising known as the Meeker Massacre. The Utes had become frustrated at Meeker's constant efforts to change them into a sedentary band of Indians, and were sullen because monies and supplies promised by a treaty with the Federal Government were long overdue. Sadly, this massacre brought an end to the Ute occupancy in Colorado, and most of them were escorted to a reservation in Utah. Today, there are some remaining Utes living in the southwestern corner of Colorado near Ignacio and Towaoc.

Left: Autumn sunset on McCall's Lake west of Longmont, with 14,256 ft. Long's Peak in the background.

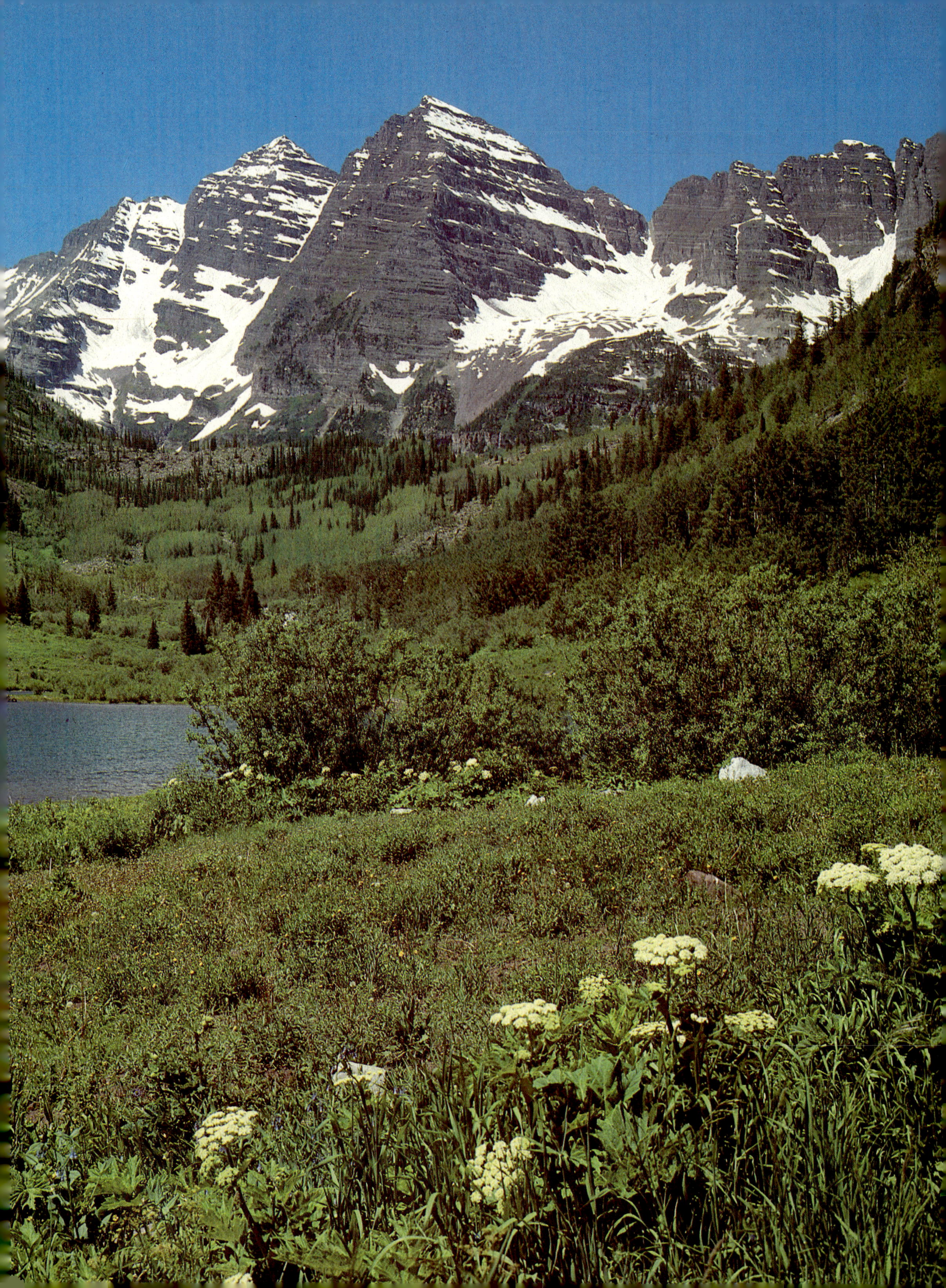

The Ute names, and names of their great leaders are permanently imprinted on the land (including Utah). Words such as "yampa", an edible root, is the name of a river; "Uncompahgre" is Colorado's longest plateau and also a valley; "Sawatch" is the loftiest section of the Continental Divide. The Great Chieftain, Ouray, has a city named after him, and his portrait is one of sixteen adorning the dome of the Capitol in Denver.

There were other Indian tribes which contributed to Colorado's kaleidoscopic history, all of them immigrants from other homelands from which they had been driven. The first plains tribes to appear were the Comanche, who were generally hated and feared by other tribes. Comanches were masterful horsethieves, raiders, and kidnappers, who made a fortune exchanging stolen goods (particularly hostages) for ammunitions, supplies, and whiskey.

Another tribe, the Kiowa, though small in number, was regarded as the most bloodthirsty of all plains Indians, killing more whites than any other tribe. For years, the Kiowa and Comanches were at war with each other, then formed an alliance and combined forces to harass white settlements for miles around. Then followed the Cheyenne and Arapaho, bitter enemies of the Kiowa and Comanche, and more wars were fought.

In 1832, the largest and most celebrated trading post was completed by the Bent and St. Vrain Company, a subsidiary of the American Fur Company. Bent's Fort, as it was called, attracted the Cheyenne, Arapaho, Kiowa, and Comanche and they frequently went there to trade goods. It was here that a great council took place in 1840 in which these tribes, deadliest of enemies, finally buried the hatchet and made peace permanently. Bent's Fort was also the trading post for the great mountain men and folk heroes of the Ol' West. Kit Carson, Jim Bridger, "Broken Hand" Fitzpatrick, Jim Baker, "Uncle Dick" Wootton, and many others came here.

Fransisco Vasquez Coronado, a sixteenth century Spaniard, pushed north from Mexico and led Spanish explorers in search of gold and silver. Other Spaniards continued to explore the territory during the next two centuries and huge land grants were taken to strengthen the Spanish frontier. Although Spain did not hesitate to claim the region as her possession, little attempt was made to colonize it. Indeed, there was gold in Colorado, but the Spaniards failed to find it. Even French fur traders went on explorations during the eighteenth century, but their influence was brief and so was their stay. Not until 1851 was the first permanent white settlement established in the town of San Luis.

After the purchase of the Louisiana Territory by the United States in 1803, Americans began to appear on the scene. The first official explorer, Lieutenant Zebulon Montgomery Pike, was dispatched to map, explore and record scientific data about the new land. He made an unsuccessful attempt at reaching the peak that now bears his name. It wasn't until 1819 that Major Stephen H. Long, leading an exploring party, succeeded in scaling the peak. During his surveys, Long also discovered Long's Peak, which was later named for him. His explorations of the high plains between the Platte and Arkansas rivers led him to call the Great Plains the "Great American Desert". Long's journeying in the region was extensive, and as a result of his reports, which declared the land uninhabitable, little attention was given to the territory for several years.

In 1842, another government explorer named Leiutenant John C. Fremont was dispatched and knowledge of the area began to spread, attracting fur traders, trappers, and frontier scouts.

Left: Maroon Bells and Lake in the springtime.

Above: The Durango-Silverton Narrow Gauge clings to a shelf as it descends the Colorado Rockies through the Las Animas River Canyon.

Right: On the Million Dollar Highway, Silverton nestles in a high mountain valley at an elevation of 9302 ft. and is surrounded by the San Juan National Forest. The mines of Silverton have produced in excess of 500 million dollars in gold, silver, and other metals.

THERE'S GOLD IN THEM THAR HILLS!

"…'there were men in every rig; hunters and trappers in buckskins; men of the Plains with belts and revolvers, in great blue cloaks, relics of the war; teamsters in leather suits; horsemen in fur coats, caps, and buffalo-hide boots; Broadway dandies in yellow kid gloves; and rich English sporting tourists, supercilious-looking."

It was 1859 before gold was finally discovered. On May 6th, to be exact, John Gregory made his great strike near present-day Central City. The editor of the New York TRIBUNE, Horace Greeley, described what he saw to his readers: "As yet the entire population of the valley—which cannot number less than 4,000, including five white women and seven squaws living with white men—sleep in tents or under booths of pine boughs, cooking and eating in the open air. I doubt that there is as yet a table or chair in these diggins…The food, like that of the plains, is restricted to a few staples—pork, hot bread, beans, and coffee forming the almost exclusive diet of the mountains; but a meat shop has just been established, on whose altar are offered up the ill-fed and well-whipped oxen who are just in from a 50-day journey across the plains." Eager gold-hunters were arriving at a rate of 500 a day, and the cry of "Pikes Peak or Bust!" became famous.

Bustling gold-dust towns of Central City, Gold Hill, Black Hawk, Cripple Creek, Boulder, Colorado City, and others made mining history. Of the thousands of gold seekers, very few found their bonanza, and by 1890 only a few permanent mining towns remained. Those who failed to find gold hurled another famous cry: "Pikes Peak Humbug!"

Concurrent with the booming mining business was Colorado's period of territorial government. In 1861 legislation provided for a governing administration to be appointed by President Lincoln, and he chose William Gilpin as the first governor. Over the next fifteen years, seven governors were appointed, but none of them lasted the four-year term...certainly a sign of instability. Nevertheless, Colorado survived and continued to make progress, and on Aug. 1, 1876 Colorado became the 38th State of the Union. In honor of the one-hundreth anniversary of the Declaration of Independence, Colorado became known as the "Centennial State."

During the 1880s and 1890s, Colorado progressed by leaps and bounds. Probably the single, most important event in its history was the construction of irrigation systems. The seeds of this development were planted during the gold rush, when it was impossible to transport enough food by wagons to feed the thousands of prospectors. Enterprising pioneers began taking water from streams and applying it to the land in order to grow crops. Agriculture and farming grew, new crops grew, and so did wealth. Buffalo herds, which had been obliterated, were replaced with sheep and cattle. Industries expanded. Cities sprouted. Automobiles, railroads and tunnels united mountains and plains.

Just for comparison, the 1870 census showed 39,864 people living in the state and by 1900 it had grown to 539,700! Colorado was flourishing.

By the early 1900's, Colorado had become a summer playground for the South and Midwest. Colorado had already established the first forest reserve, White River National Forest, in 1891, but the need to preserve the beauty and history of the region was continuously recognized. Enos Mills, with tireless ambition wrote: "Without parks and outdoor life all that is best in civilization will be smothered." Two more national parks were created, the Mesa Verde in 1906 and the Rocky Mountain in 1915, and four national monuments were set aside. Today, there are millions of preserved acres, enough to make Enos Mills a proud man.

Far left: In Silverton, the terminal of the Durango to Silverton Narrow Gauge Railroad can be seen in the distance.

Above left: Memory of the mother lode.

Above right: Nevadaville City Hall

Left: Ghost mill in the Rockies.

27

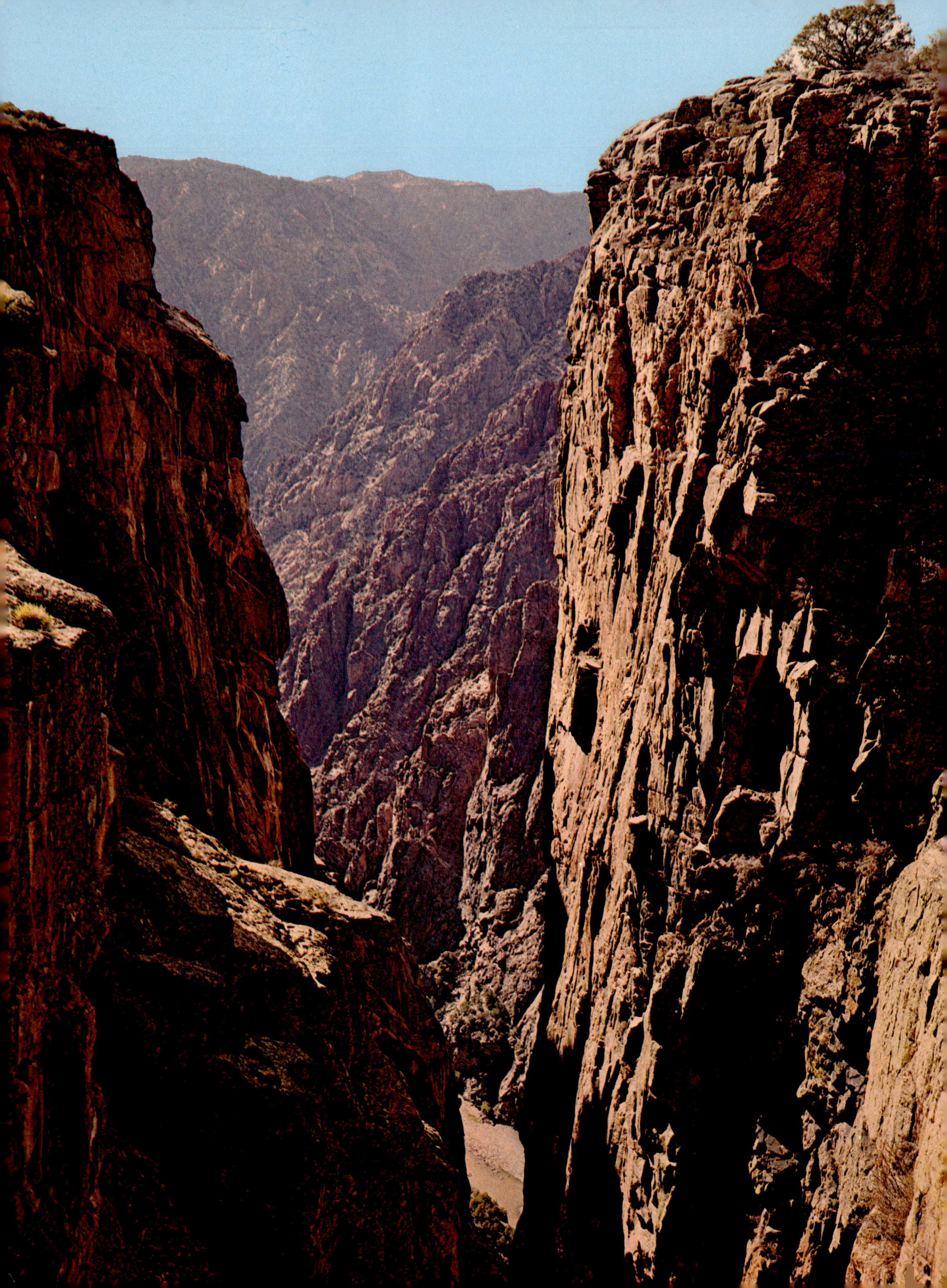

NATIONAL PARKS AND MONUMENTS

"He who feels the spell of the wild, the rhythmic melody of falling water, the echoes among the crags, the bird songs, the wind in the pines...is in tune with the universe."

Enos Mills

Indeed, the late Enos Mills should be given credit for much of the popularity of this region. He spent his life making friends with nature and always wrote glowingly of what he saw. He was a die-hard campaigner for preservation, and he succeeded.

Perhaps one of the most outstanding examples of natural landscape, in such extraordinary variety, lying within a very small area, is Rocky Mountain National Park. Its 405 square miles contains a remarkable chain of mountain peaks, moraines, canyons, alpine valleys, glacial lakes, and hundreds of streams. Over 700 species of wild flowers carpet forests, valleys, and high mountain meadows. It is a wildlife sanctuary for the Rocky Mountain big horn sheep (Colorado's state animal), elk, mule deer, beaver, golden eagle, ptarmigan and many other wild creatures. For the photographer, sportsman, hiker or vacationer...THIS is the place to be.

Rocky Mountain National Park actually includes a large portion of the Front Range of the Rockies. There are 65 peaks rising more than 10,000 feet, and 16 more which exceed 12,000 feet. Long's Peak, at a height of 14,255 feet, dominates the park.

Winding through this more than 226,000-acre wilderness is a modern highway...the most important road in the park. Trail Ridge Road runs past chasms thousands of feet deep and climbs high above the timberline, twisting its way through the wind-combed tundra which in summer is covered with exquisite tiny wildflowers. Although modern Trail Ridge Road reflects an outstanding engineering achievement, the Trail was in use long before the first white settler came to the present park area. The Utes and the Arapahoes were the first to discover this passage across "The Great Divide". For most of its length, the road follows the old trail, and where they do separate, the former pathway is still discernible, especially near the Gore Range Overlook, as it winds down toward Milner Pass. The first automobile traveled the road in September of 1920. At that time, the eastern portion of the road followed the Fall River Road route to the top of Fall River Pass. In 1932 the road was rerouted on the east side to become Trail Ridge Road. This highway links the eastern and western sections of Rocky Mountain National Park. From high points along the road, one sees lush valleys and wondrous mountain crests as well as glistening rivers reflecting the Colorado sun. To the east, the Great Plains blend into the hazy horizon; to the west, the sky-probing peaks of the Never Summer Range and the headwaters basin of the powerful Colorado River are clearly visible. Snow usually closes Trail Ridge Road from late October until late May.

Left: This spine-chilling view down Black Canyon includes Dragon Point on the right and a glimpse of the river below.

Overleaf: Bear Lake in Rocky Mountain National Park.

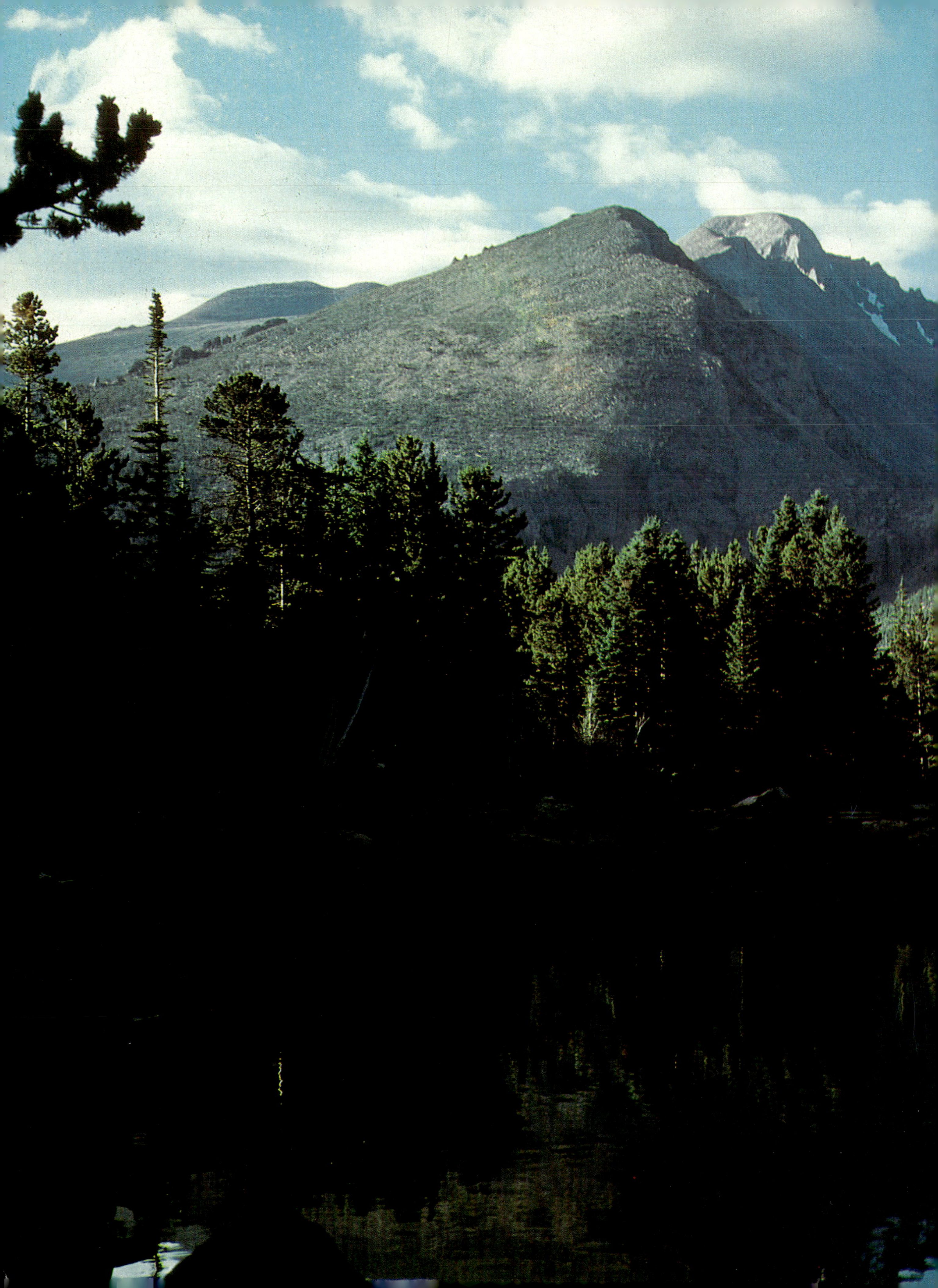

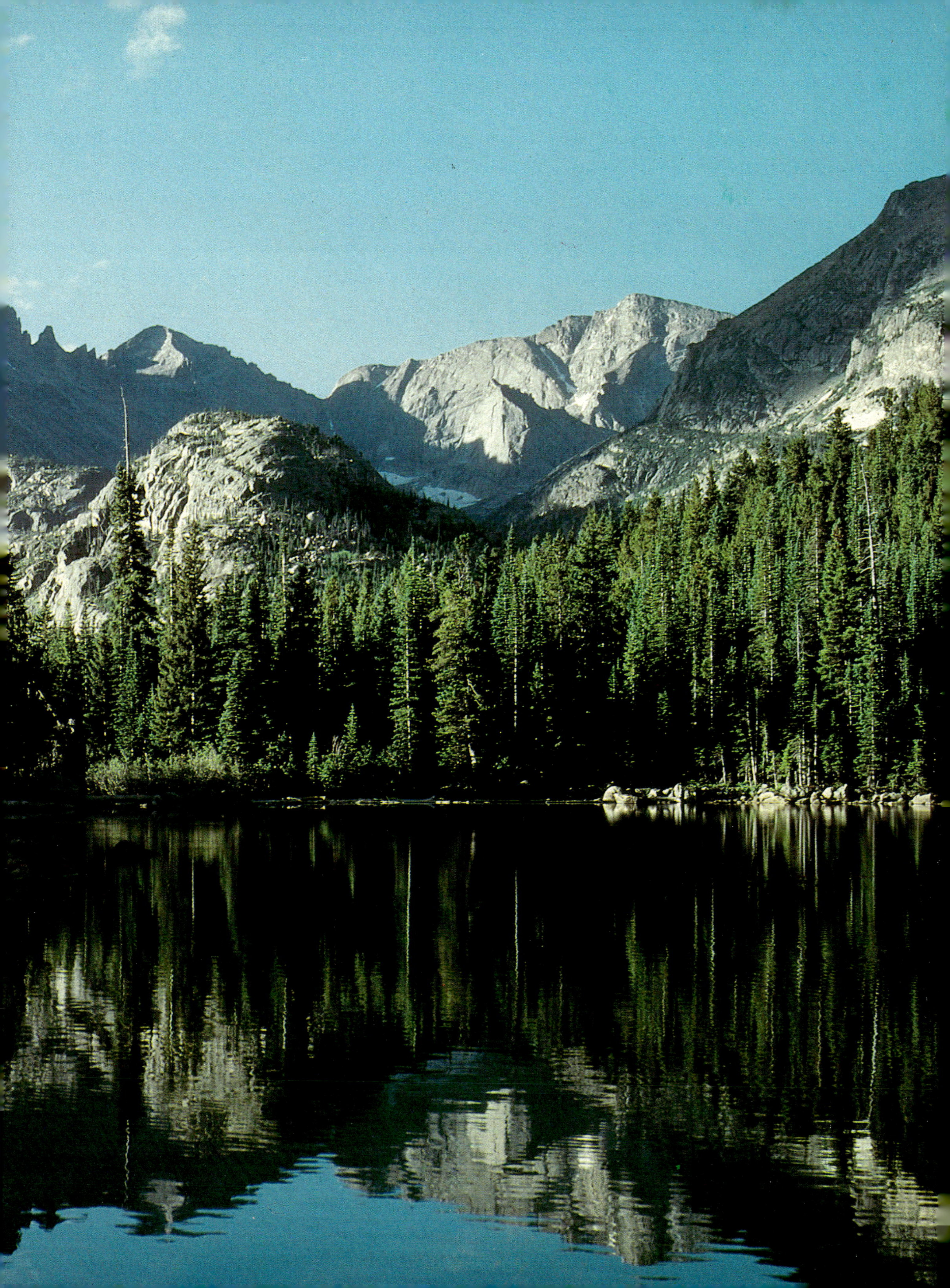

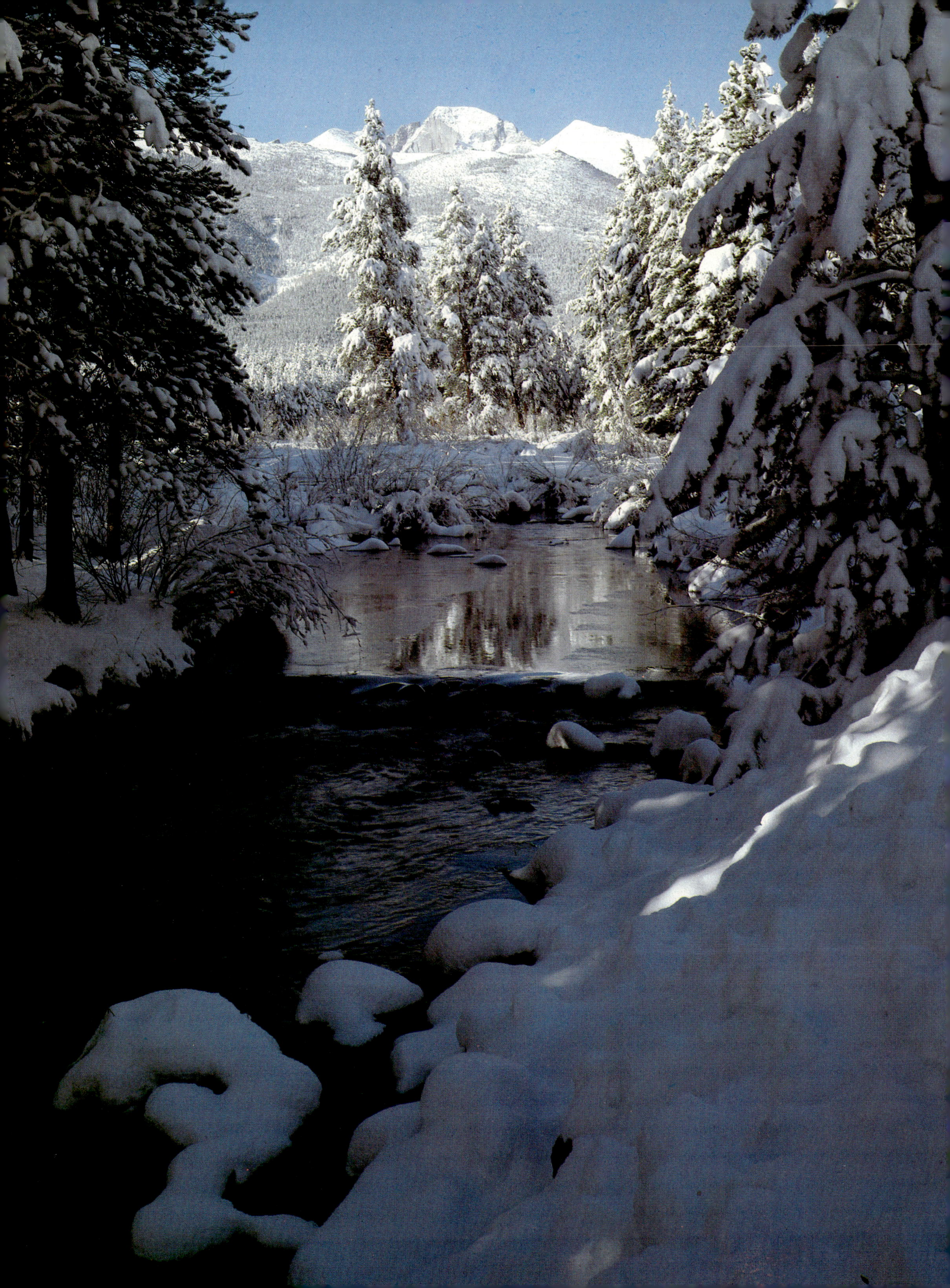

The village of Estes Park is the eastern gateway to Rocky Mountain National Park. Its year-round population is about 4,500, but in summer the place is bustling with tourists eager to visit the park and to enjoy the many resort hotels, dude ranches, and campgrounds in the area.

Joel Estes first settled with his family in the huge rugged valley amid the eastern slopes of the Rockies in 1860. The previous year he had visited the region and had fallen in love with its beauty and isolation. When two other families moved into the area, Estes moved out, complaining of too many people.

The Peak-to-Peak Highway (made up of State Highways 7, 72, and 119), connecting Estes Park to Central City and U.S. Highway 6, roughly parallels the eastern boundary of the Rocky Mountain National Park. The road leads to Long's Peak Campground and the Wild Basin section of the park. From vantage points along this scenic highway, one can see Rock Cut, Twin Sisters Peaks, Red Rock Lake, Saint Malo Chapel with Mount Meeker (13,911 feet) providing a dramatic background, and the serene beauty of one of the Wild Basin's exquisite meadows—contrasting splendidly with the majesty of Mount Copeland (13,176 feet).

Far left: Glacier Creek and Long's Peak in Rocky Mountain National Park

Left: The Saint Malo Chapel, located on the Peak-to-Peak Highway between Estes Park and Allen's Park.

Overleaf: Mount Meeker (left) and Long's Peak (right) in Colorado's Front Range as seen from the Estes Park area.

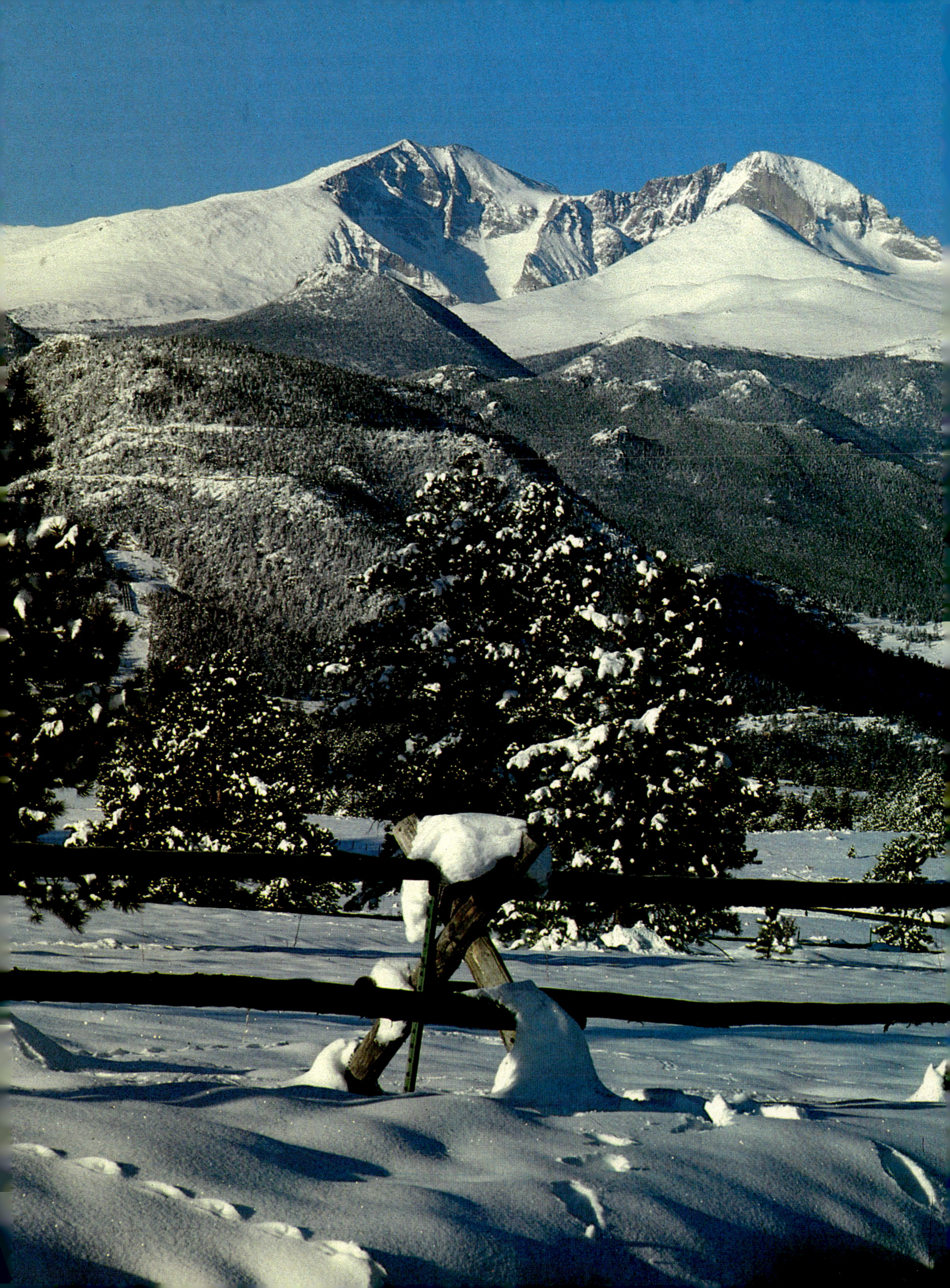

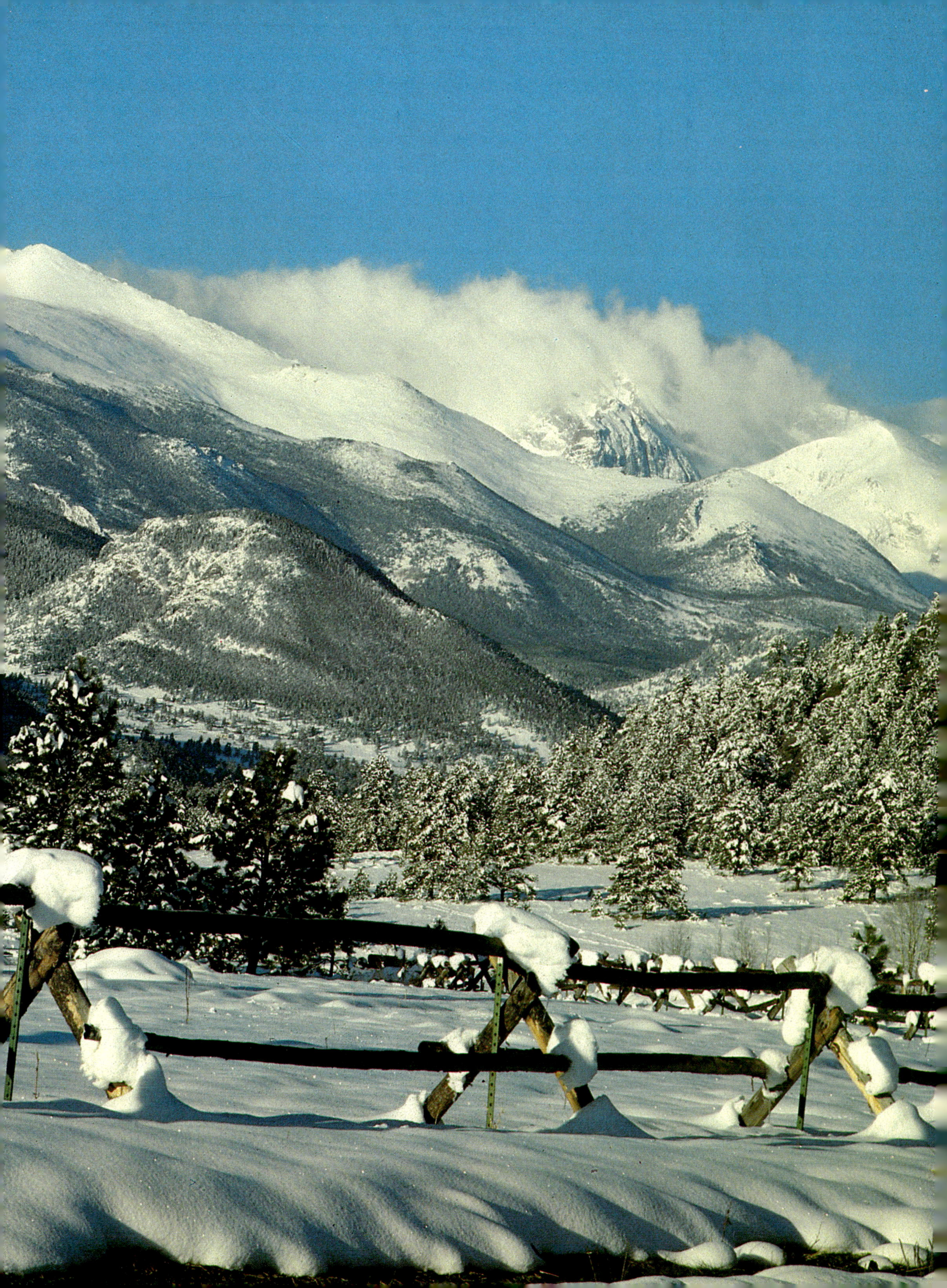

Left: Trail Ridge Road in Rocky Mountain National Park.

Below: Sunrise over Dillon Reservoir.

Right: Pine trees frame the beautiful Loch in the Glacier Gorge area of Colorado's Rocky Mountain National Park. Taylor Glacier is the snow field area in the background.

Overleaf: Shadow Mountain, Grand Lake.

The Bear Lake area of the park offers a breathtaking assemblage of high country variety for photographer, hiker, rider, and fisherman alike. Located about ten miles southwest of Estes Park, Bear Lake country is the starting point to four other lakes in the park—Nymph, Dream, Emerald, and Haiyaha. Bierstadt Lake and Flattop Mountain are also in the same locale.

Glacier Gorge and Loch Vale are two other unique areas. The gorge is bordered by some of the highest mountains in the park. Dominating the immediate landscape are Storm Peak, Long's Peak, the Key Board of the Winds, and Pagota Peak. At the bottom of this glacial valley are Mills Lake, Jewel Lake, and Black Lake. Loch Vale is not far from Glacier Gorge Junction, neighbored by small cliffs and twisted trees that create a quiet beauty The valley itself affords a splendid view of Taylor Glacier. Beyond the lake lie Sky Pond and the Lake of Glass.

Nymph Lake is a photographer's dream. Framed by Glacier Gorge and Hallett Peak, its surface covered with lilypads, it presents a breathless beauty.

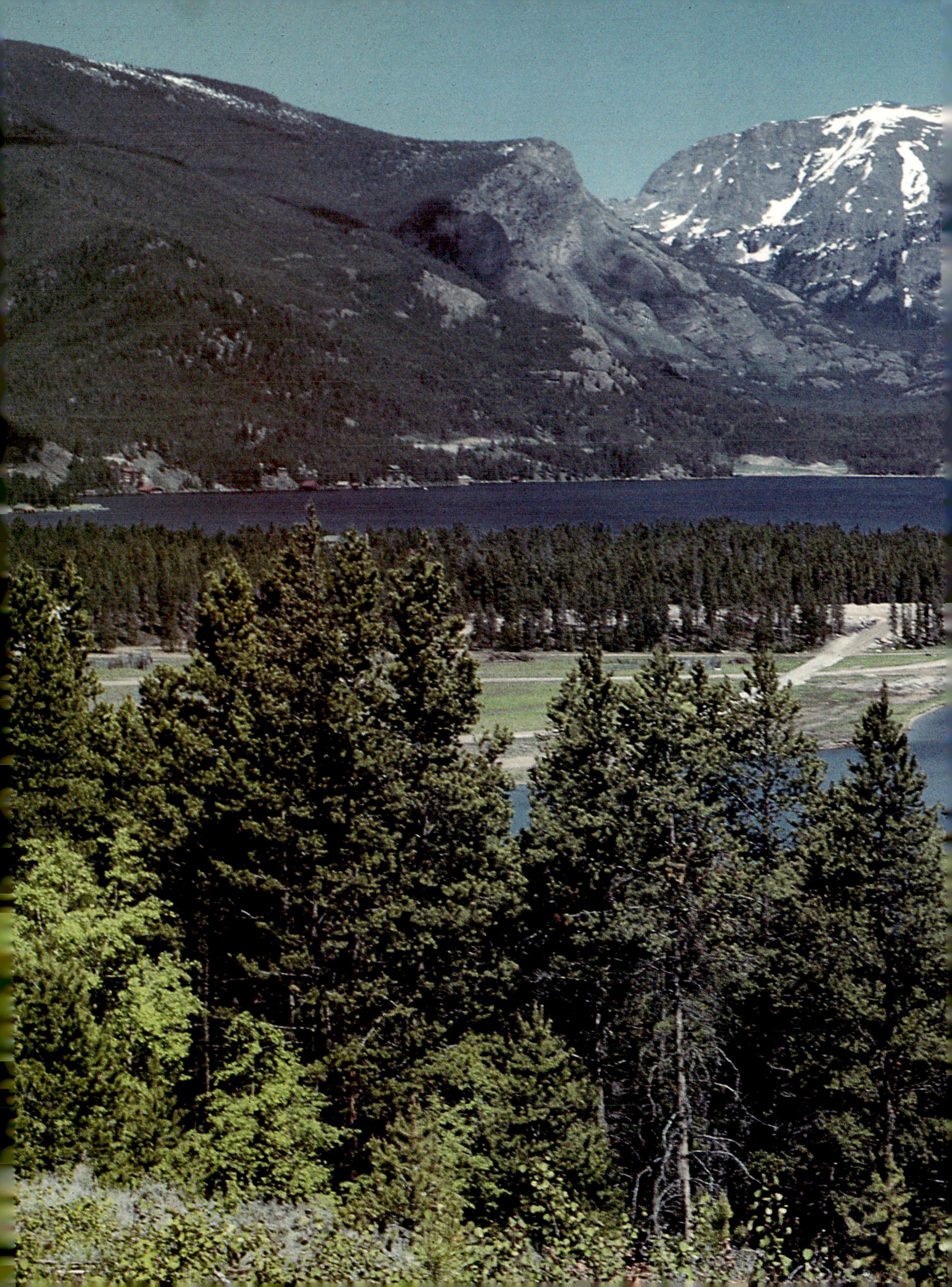

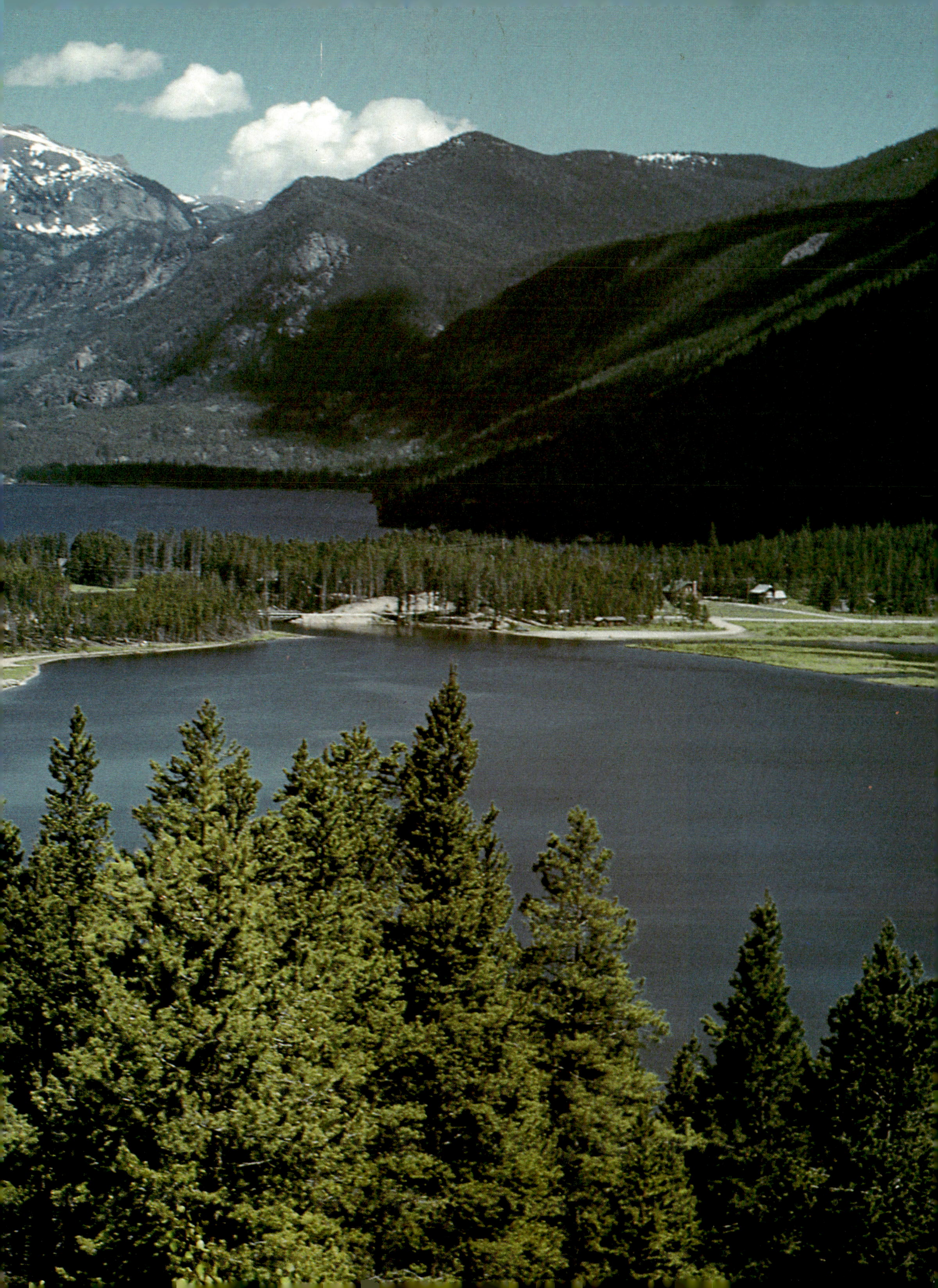

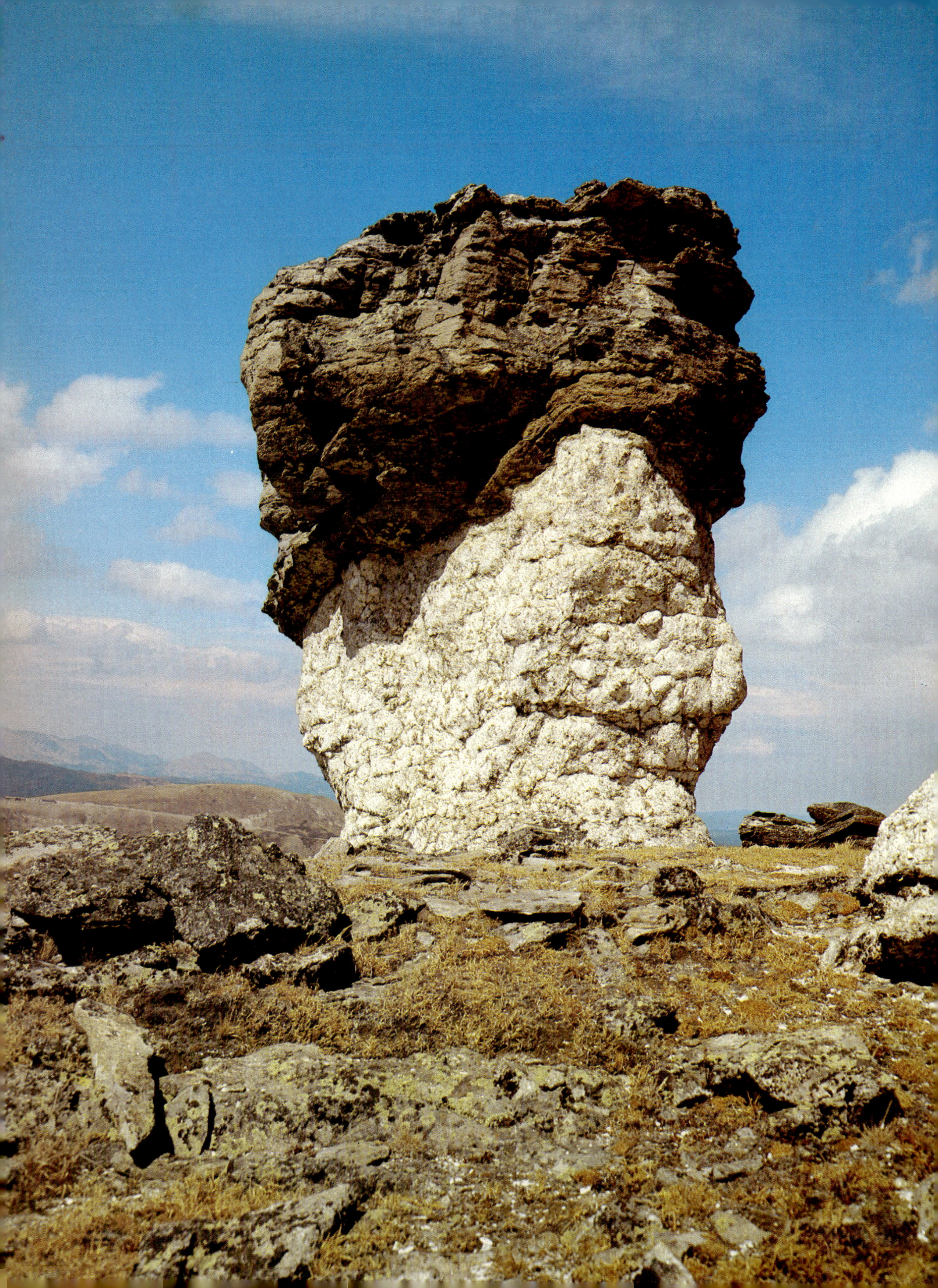

There are three active glaciers in the Bear Lake area—Taylor Glacier, Andrews Glacier, and Tyndall Glacier. These reminders of the Ice Age that prevailed more than a million years ago contribute to the magnificent spectacle of the region.

Bordering Rocky Mountain National Park on the southwest is Arapahoe National Recreation Area, whose Grand Lake is the largest natural lake in Colorado. Grand Lake and the manmade reservoirs Shadow Mountain Lake and Lake Granby comprise the "Great Lakes" of the state. Both reservoirs were created to gather waters from the Colorado River Valley on the western slope of the Divide to the Big Thompson River drainage on the eastern slope. This water flows through the 13.1-mile Adams Tunnel that originates at the east end of Grand Lake, passes beneath the great peaks in Rocky Mountain National Park, and emerges a few miles south of Estes Park. Grand Lake is 8,380 feet above sea level.

With intriguing Mount Baldy rising to 10,205 feet to the southeast, Grand Lake provides an ideal setting for boating and fishing. The lake is the highest registered yacht anchorage in the world. The "Legend of Grand Lake" by Judge Joseph Wescott, the first permanent white setter in the area, begins with the words: "White man, pause and gaze around,/For we tread now on haunted ground!" Grand Lake was called "Spirit Lake" by the Arapaho Indians. The ghosts of the region became part of legendary history following a fierce battle between the Ute mountain tribe and a marauding party of Arapaho and Cheyenne warriors. During the fighting, the women and small children of the Utes were placed on a raft and sent to the middle of the lake as a protective measure. An abrupt storm capsized the raft, drowning all aboard. According to legend, on a summer morning ghostly figures rise from the lake, and in the dead of winter the moaning of the Ute women and children can be heard coming from beneath the ice.

During the gold rush days of the late 1870's and early 1880's, Grand Lake was the region's center of activity. Even though no mines were in its immediate vicinity, the young village prospered as a supply and trading base for Lulu City, Gaskill, Teller City, Dutchtown, and Pearl. Almost every trace of these towns is gone, but one can still view the remains of Lulu City.

Another very significant preserve is Colorado's Mesa Verde National Park. It includes 50,275 acres of mesa lands and canyons which contain many ancient cliff dwellings and pueblos of the earliest inhabitants. (See page 15).

Mesa Verde means green table in Spanish. It is a 15 mile by 8 mile mound of earth and rock which rises as much as 2,000 feet from Montezuma Valley on the north, and 1,000 feet on the south. Within this area are approximately 350 cliff dwellings, several hundred Basket Maker pit dwellings and 400 mesa top pueblos. One of the largest is Spruce Tree House, a village with 122 rooms which may have had up to 200 inhabitants. It is estimated this village was built somewhere between 1230 and 1274 A.D.

Left: One of the Mushroom Rocks along the Tundra Nature Trail above Rock Cut in Rocky Mountain National Park. These outcrops contain some of the oldest rock in the park.

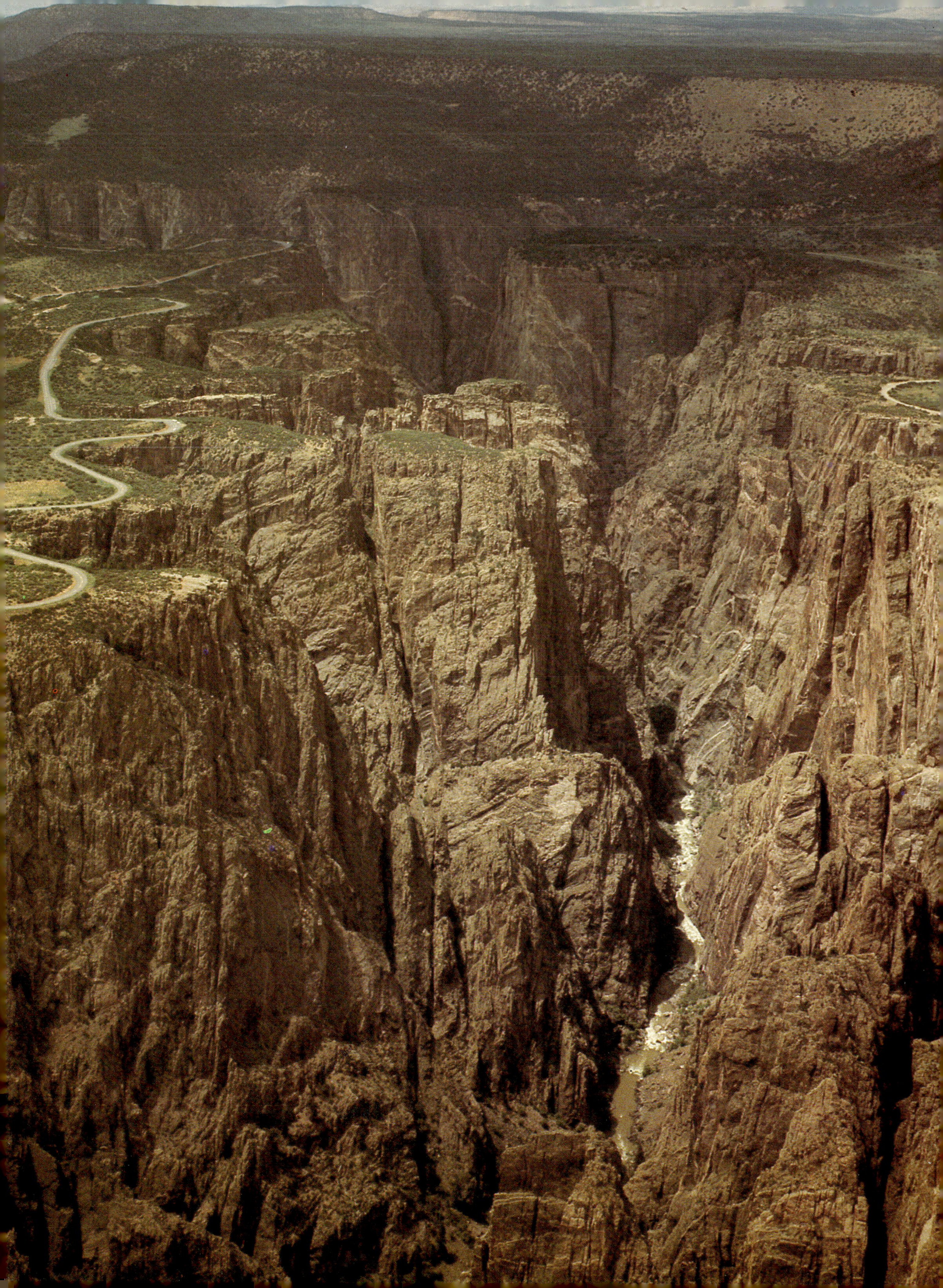

Cliff dwellings, pueblos, and rock towers are also found around the "Four Corners" area—the southwestern point of Colorado.

Black Canyon of the Gunnison National Monument is probably the wildest, deepest, rockiest, darkest canyon in the world. This national monument is a 10-mile strip of the most spectacular portion of the 50-mile canyon through granite by the Gunnison River. Black Canyon is located near Montrose in the western part of the state. In places, its sheer walls reach a height of 2,425 feet. The canyon itself reaches a depth of 3,200 feet, and although the distance between its rims may be 1,300 feet wide, it is often no more than 40 feet wide at the bottom. The black walls have pink mica in them, and looking down from the higher elevations one is able to see the sudsing white stream below; sunlight glinting from the mica creates an eerie background. The canyon is so narrow and so dark in spots that it is said that in broad daylight, looking up from the bottom, one can see the stars in the sky.

The first white men to explore the canyon area where the Gunnison River has cut a deep gorge in one of the earth's oldest granite rocks were Spaniards coming from Santa Fe in 1765 in search of gold. For today's explorers, there are descending Indian trails that the careful visitor can try, and there are well organized boat trips, but any other routes of descent should be left to experienced climbers. The Black Canyon of the Gunnison National Monument is closed by snow in winter.

Unique among the state's national monuments is the Colorado National Monument in the central section west of the Rockies. Established as a national monument in 1911, the area occupies some 17,693 acres and contains many deep canyons with extraordinarily eroded red sandstone walls. Situated west of Grand Junction, the national monument offers exciting views from Serpent's Trail, Rimrock Drive, and Cold Shivers Point.

Cliff dwelling ruins and dinosaur remains have been discovered here, but one of the amazing features of the region is the large number of rock monoliths distributed throughout the area. One of these, Independence Rock, reaches upward for 500 feet. The canyons and hills are filled with these red and white sandstone columns of fantastic sizes and shapes. Besides Independence Rock, there are Devil's Kitchen, Coke Oven, and Window Rock that are of particular interest. The monument area overlooks the Colorado River and its broad fertile valley of orchards and farms. Bison, deer, and elk roam the region, protected by the National Park Service. Meadows of wildflowers and pine and juniper forests surround the mountains. Not far away, on the other side of Grand Junction, is Grand Mesa, the largest flat-topped mountain in the United States. Two-mile high Grand Mesa is adorned with sparkling lakes.

Dinosaur National Monument stretches its 206,760 acres of untouched frontierland across northwestern Colorado and northeastern Utah. Much of the scenic beauty here resulted from erosion by the Green and Yampa rivers. The sides of the narrow canyons through which these rivers rush are oddly carved cliffs made of sandstone and reaching a height of 2,000 feet.

In the Utah section of the Dinosaur National Monument, great beds of dinosaur fossils have been discovered, some as long as 84 feet. Steamboat Rock, sculpted out of layers of sandstone by the merging of the two rivers, is now 700 feet above the surface that once covered it. Fragile dinosaur bones are still being gingerly removed from the huge quarry. The bones were imbedded in the hillside about 1,000,000 years ago. The reconstructed skeletons are presently housed in a museum in Jensen, Utah. There are also Indian pictographs in this monument that may be well over a thousand years old.

Left: This aerial view of Black Canyon of the Gunnison is toward the west showing the Gunnison River and the Painted Wall are at the far end of the gorge, some 2,400 feet deep. Rim drives and overlooks afford splendid scenic views of this great wild canyon.

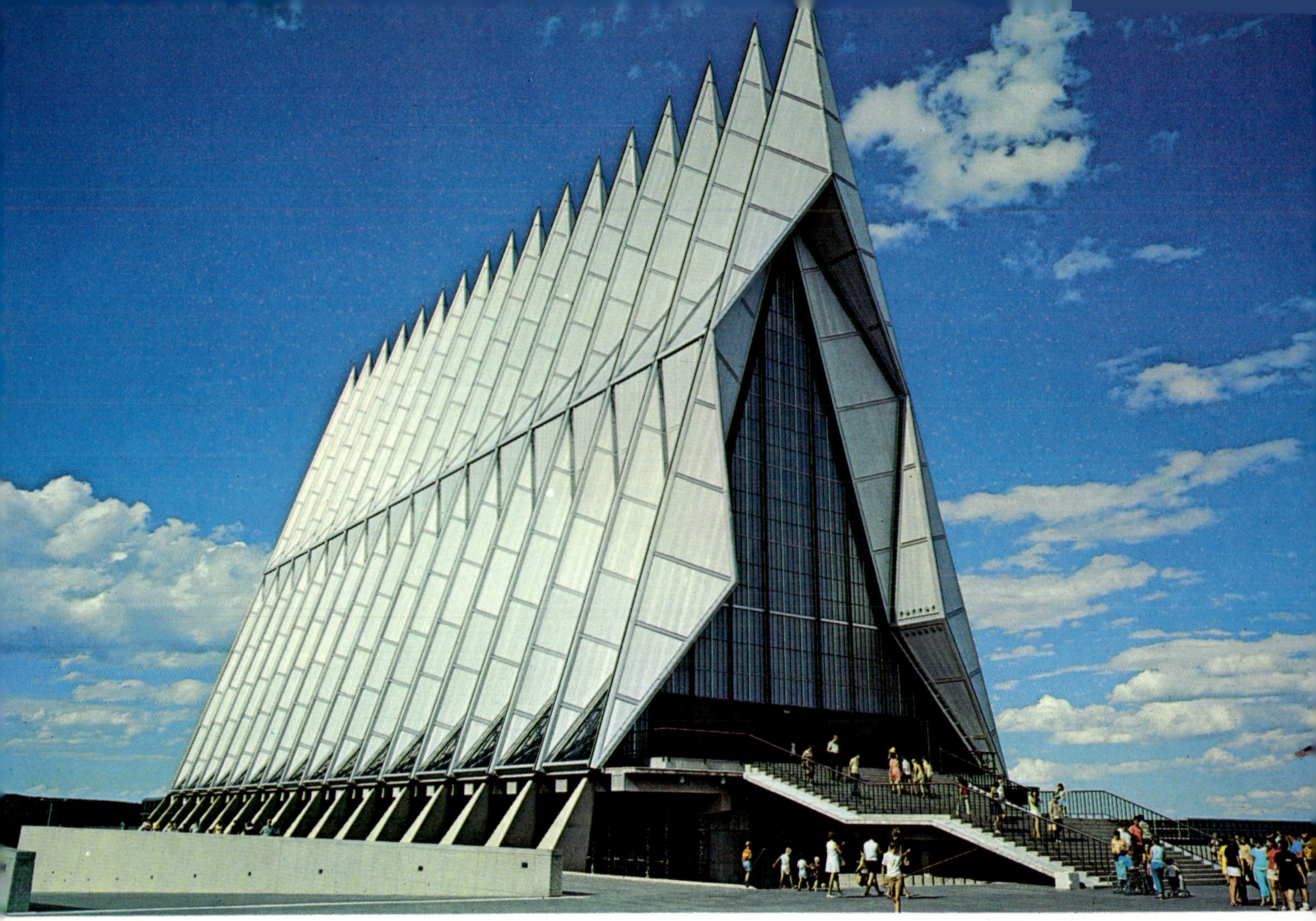
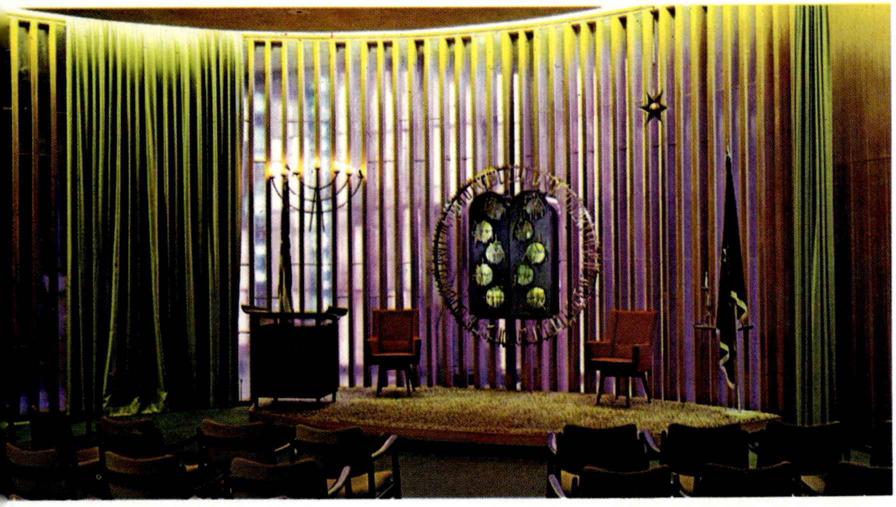
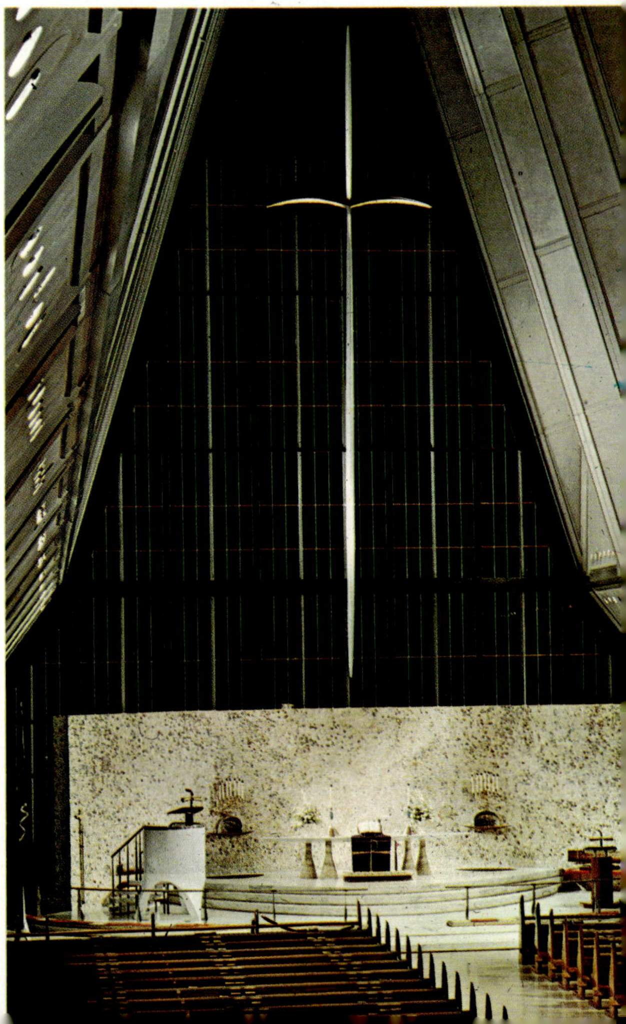
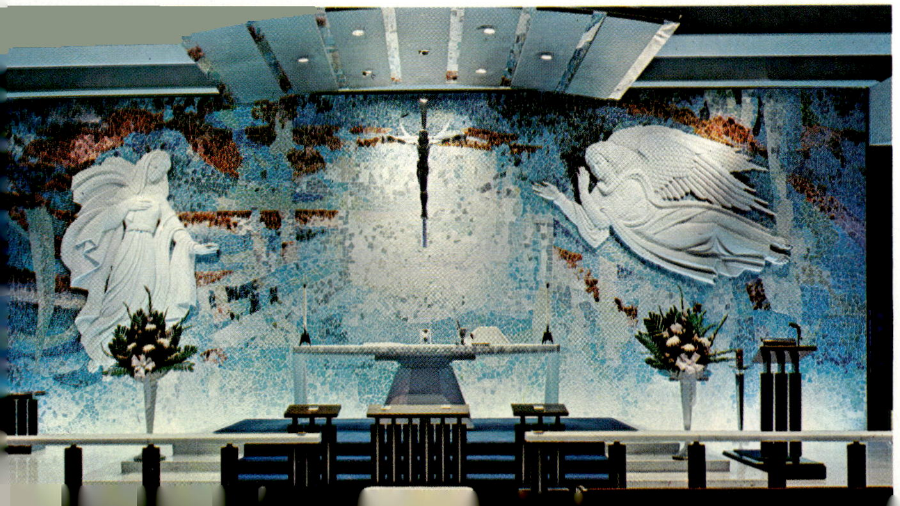

Northeast of Alamosa, on the western slopes of the Sangre de Cristo Mountains and a thousand miles from the nearest ocean, are huge sand dunes that attain heights of 1,000 feet above the valley floor. They are some of the biggest and highest sand dunes in the United States. In 1932 the area was established as the Great Sand Dunes National Monument. Exhibits of the dunes' development and history are on display at the Visitors' Center.

The famous dunes extend for ten miles, and their sands are thought to be the residue of a geologic sea that once covered the area. The wild winds blew the sands to the base of the neighboring mountains. The region includes 36,740 acres of vari-colored sands that lie in the ever shifting waves and rolls in the San Luis Valley.

Today, the wind still sculpts the finely pulverized sand into mutating hills, valleys, and plains. Radiating the warmth of sun striking hot sand, the dunes can be seen for 70 miles. Color and mood shift with the sun's angle, and lengthening shadows change the dunes from their rosy hues to cooler violets and mauves. At times, these dunes produce some of the most amazing displays of lightning in America. The wind joins with the heat rising from the sand to create gigantic thunderstorms accompanied by fantastic bolts of lightning. Close by is Medano Creek that flows for only a few months each year.

West of Cortez, on the Utah border, are other remains of ancient cliff dwellings, pueblos, and rock towers in Hovenweep National Monument. These prehistoric residences apparently were constructed by a people similar to the tribe that built the homes in Mesa Verde. This monument was established in 1923 and contains 505 acres.

Florissant Fossil Beds National Monument, one-half mile south of Florissant, in Teller County, is a 6,000-acre tract that was once covered by a lake during prehistoric times. About 35,000,000 years ago, volcanoes erupting violently filled the lake with lava and ash; today we see the perfectly formed fossils of insects, seeds, and leaves that flourished before the eruptions. There are also stands of petrified Sequoia stumps.

At the base of Pikes Peak are Manitou Springs and Colorado Springs. Just north of Colorado Springs is the newest service academy—the Air Force Academy—built in 1954. Resplendent with lovely green lawns and modern buildings, the campus provides a dramatic setting for that futuristic edifice of silvery metal and glass, the Academy Chapel. The multi-faith chapel has seventeen spires that soar 150 feet into the Colorado skies.

Left above: U.S. Air Force Academy Cadet Chapel.

Center far left: Jewish Chapel

Bottom far left: Catholic Chapel

Bottom left: Protestant Chapel

Left: Adjacent to heavily forested Sangre de Cristo Mountains, dunes are continually shifted and piled as high as 1000 feet by the tireless wind.

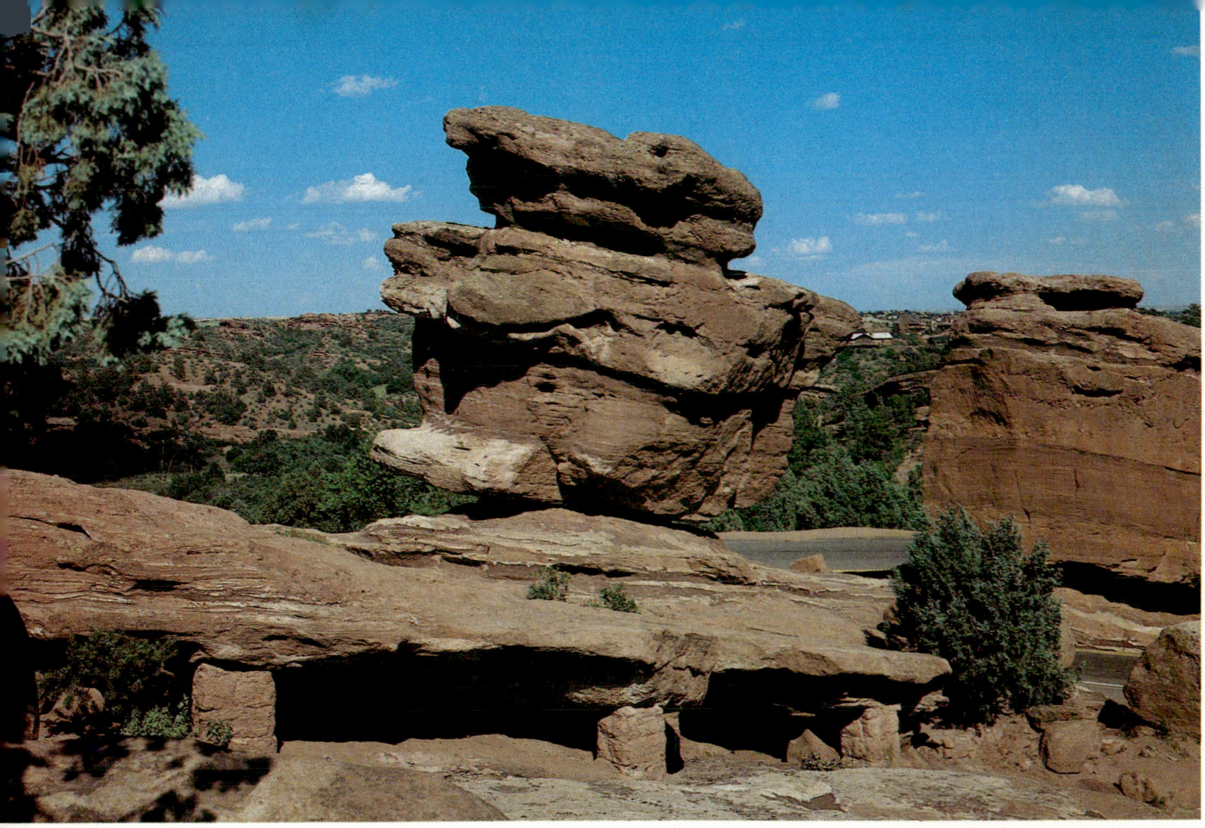
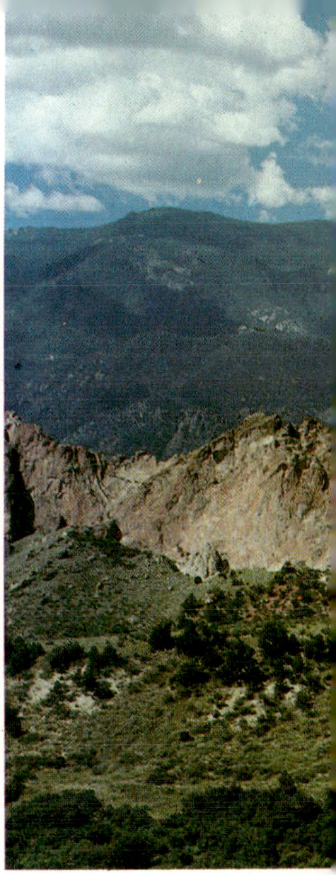
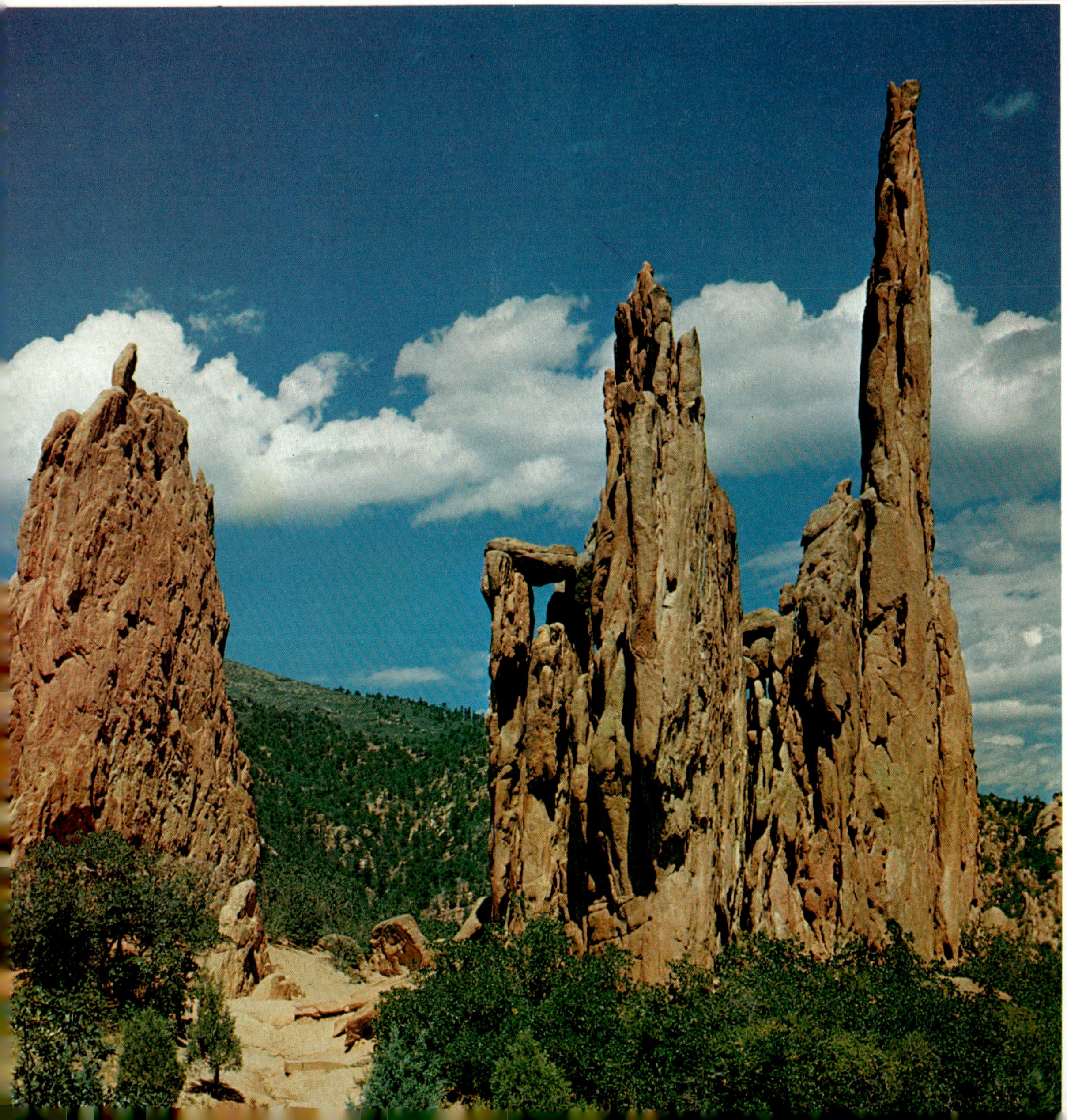
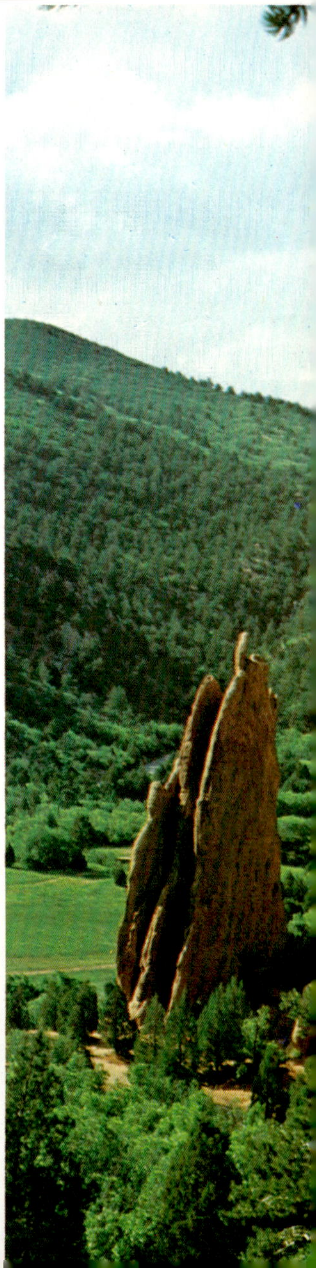

Upper left: Balanced Rock

Lower left: Montezuma's Castle

Above and left: Panoramic vista of the Garden of the Gods from the south. In the Pikes Peak Region.

Overleaf:
Garden of the Gods.

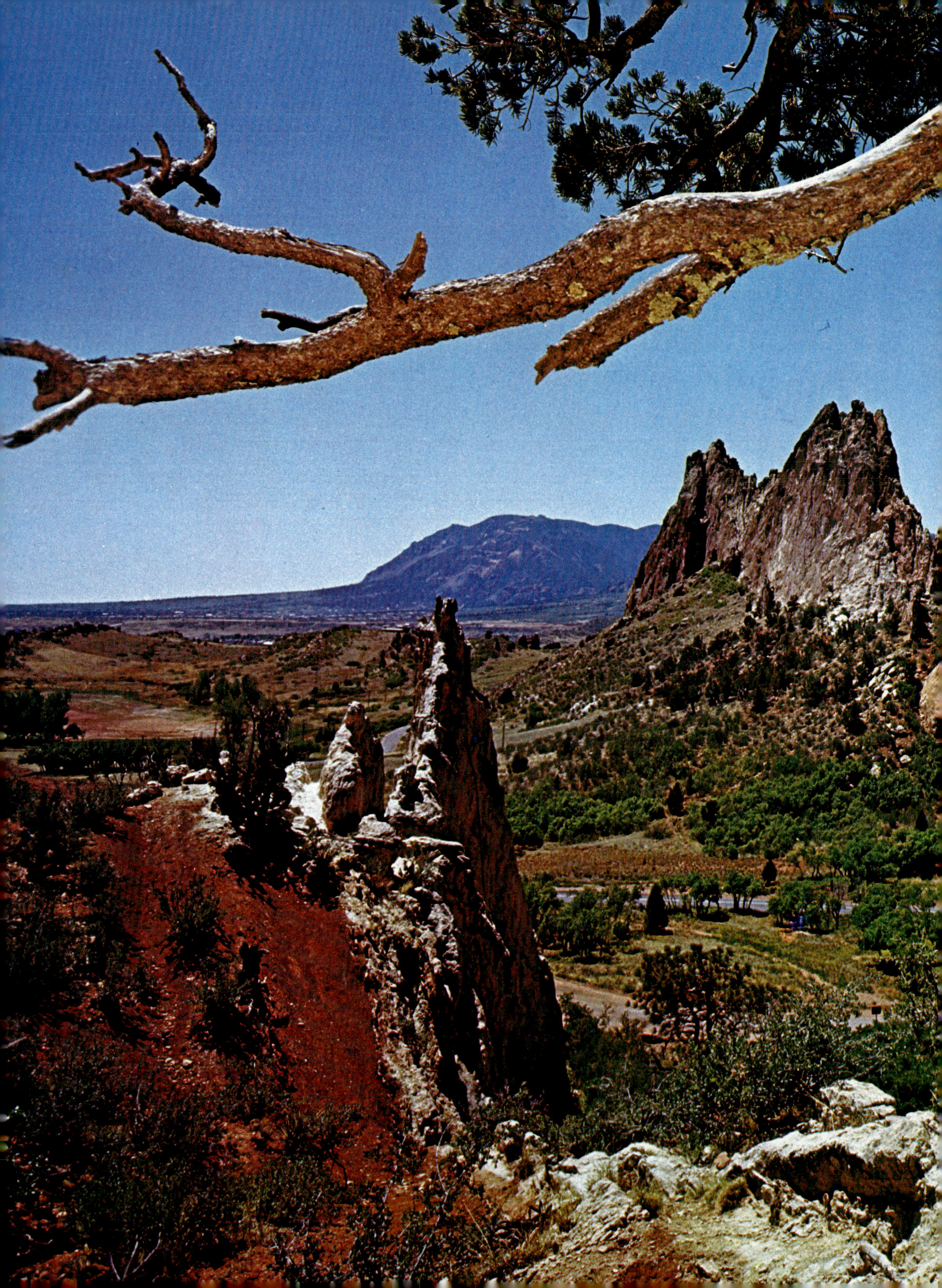

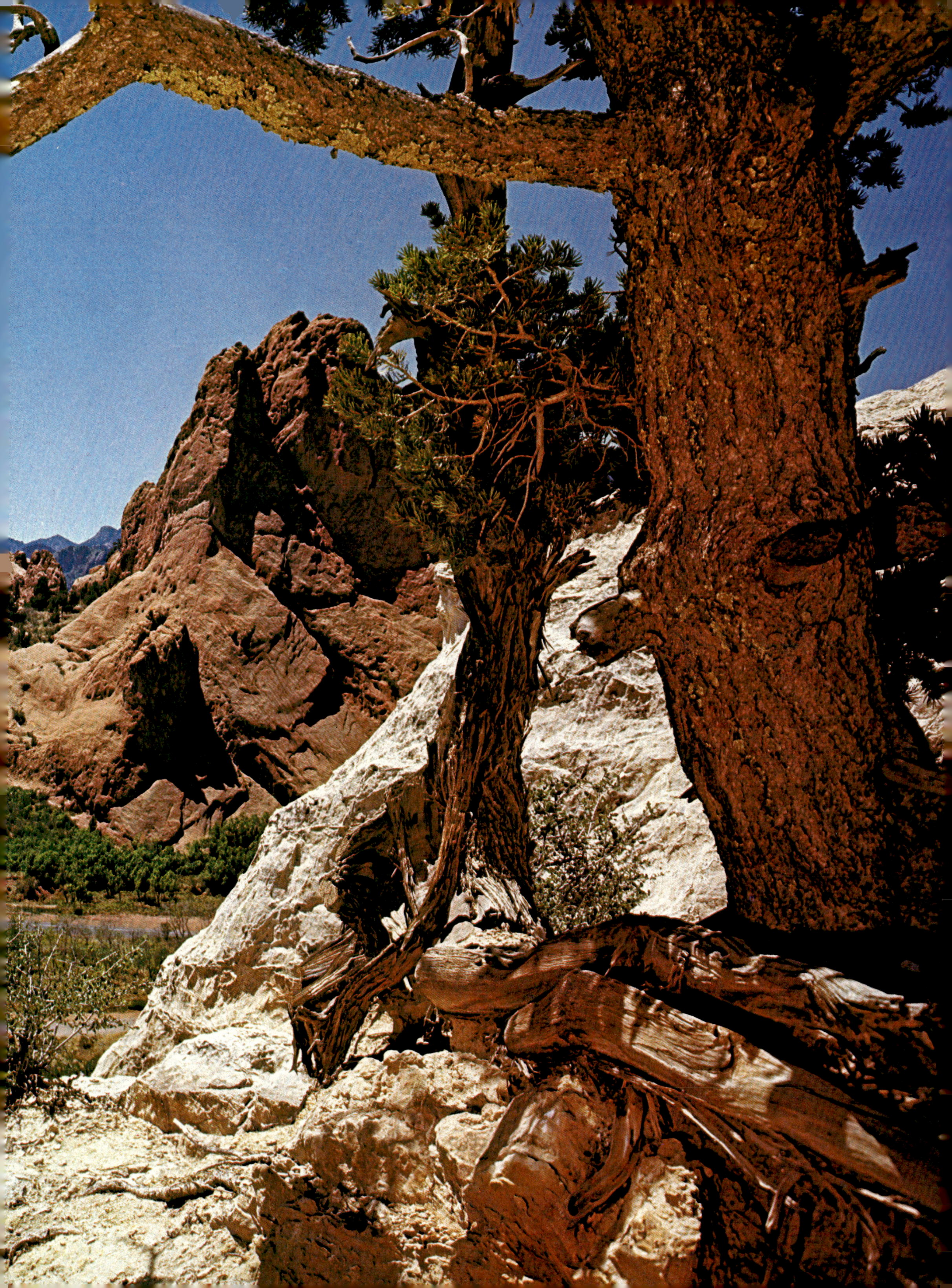

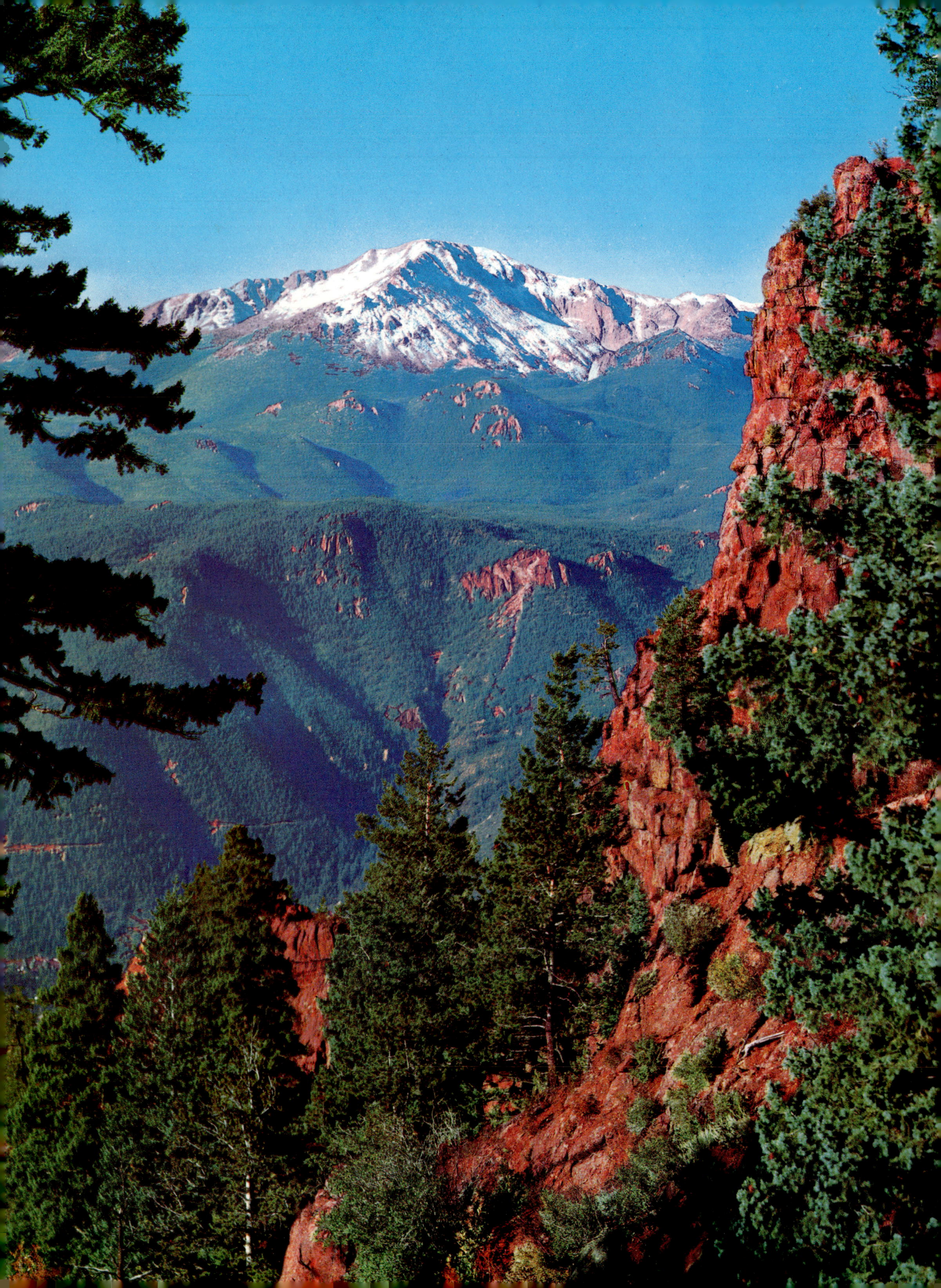

About fifteen miles southwest of Denver, near Golden, is the unique Park of the Red Rocks, a vertical amphitheater that seats 8,300, standing between two towering red promontories. One of the stone formations resembles the prow of a ship and is called Shiprock; the other is known as Creation Rock. Easter Sunrise Services are held in the theater portion of the park, as well as summer concerts and other entertainments.

The numerous reservoir regions throughout the state also provide park and recreation areas, especially the Dillon Reservoir Recreation Area. Then there are the mountain regions whose eleven National Forests contain a total of 13,714,353 acres. Some of these forests have been set aside by the Federal Government for the protection of the watersheds, for timber conservation, and for development of these great forest resources. Besides encompassing the Red Rocks Park, the Denver Mountain Parks also include Lookout Mountain Park (the location of Buffalo Bill's grave), Dedisse Park, Echo Lake Park, Genesee Park, Corwina Park, Daniels park, and Bergen Park. A side trip from Bergen Park to Echo Lake, Summit Lake, and the top of Mt. Evans, which is the highest auto roadway in the world, is an unforgetable adventure.

But perhaps the most spectacular of all these natural attractions is the Garden of the Gods, covering some 950 acres in the northwest corner of Colorado Springs at the foot of Pikes Peak. It is a natural park, with deep-red and white sandstone formations of gargantuan size scattered throughout the acres of small forests and green meadows that define the region. Some of the rock shapes are truly grotesque. The Gateway Rocks are two giant red masses, 330 feet high, that embrace the park's entrance. Other notable formations are Kissing Camels and Montezuma's Castle. The Garden of the Gods has been part of the municipal park system since 1909, and with its unusual rock formations resembles a playground for superhuman beings. Easter Sunrise Services have been held at the Gateway Rocks.

Looking up from the entrance to the Garden of the Gods, one can see the 14,110-foot summit of Pikes Peak, the best known of Colorado's titans. As the sun moves, shadows cast a purplish tint to the snow on top of the famous peak. Although it isn't the highest mountain in the state, Pikes Peak is so situated that it has a commanding view of many other mountains in the vicinity. It was the view from Pikes Peak that inspired Katharine Lee Bates to compose the words to "America the Beautiful"!

Far left: Pikes Peak.

Left: View of Auto Highway which twists and turns to summit of famous Pikes Peak, Alt. 14,110 ft.

Left: Will Rogers Memorial Shrine in Colorado Springs was erected by Spencer Penrose in memory of Will Rogers. This beautiful memorial on Cheyenne Mountain attracts thousands of visitors who enjoy a magnificent view of the Pikes Peak Region.

Below left: Night view of famous Seven Falls in South Cheyenne Cañon, Colorado Springs. During the summer and for a week at Christmas, not only the falls but the whole cañon is illuminated at night to create a fairyland of colored light throughout the cañon. The Falls drop in seven cascades, more than 300 feet.

Below: A thrilling experience for visitors to the Pikes Peak Area is the trip up the Mt. Manitou Incline Railway to the 9,455 foot summit.

Right: Snow Covered Pikes Peak, Alt. 14,110 ft., as seen looking through the Gateway to the Garden of the Gods.

Overleaf: The Yampa River flowing through the Dinosaur National Monument.

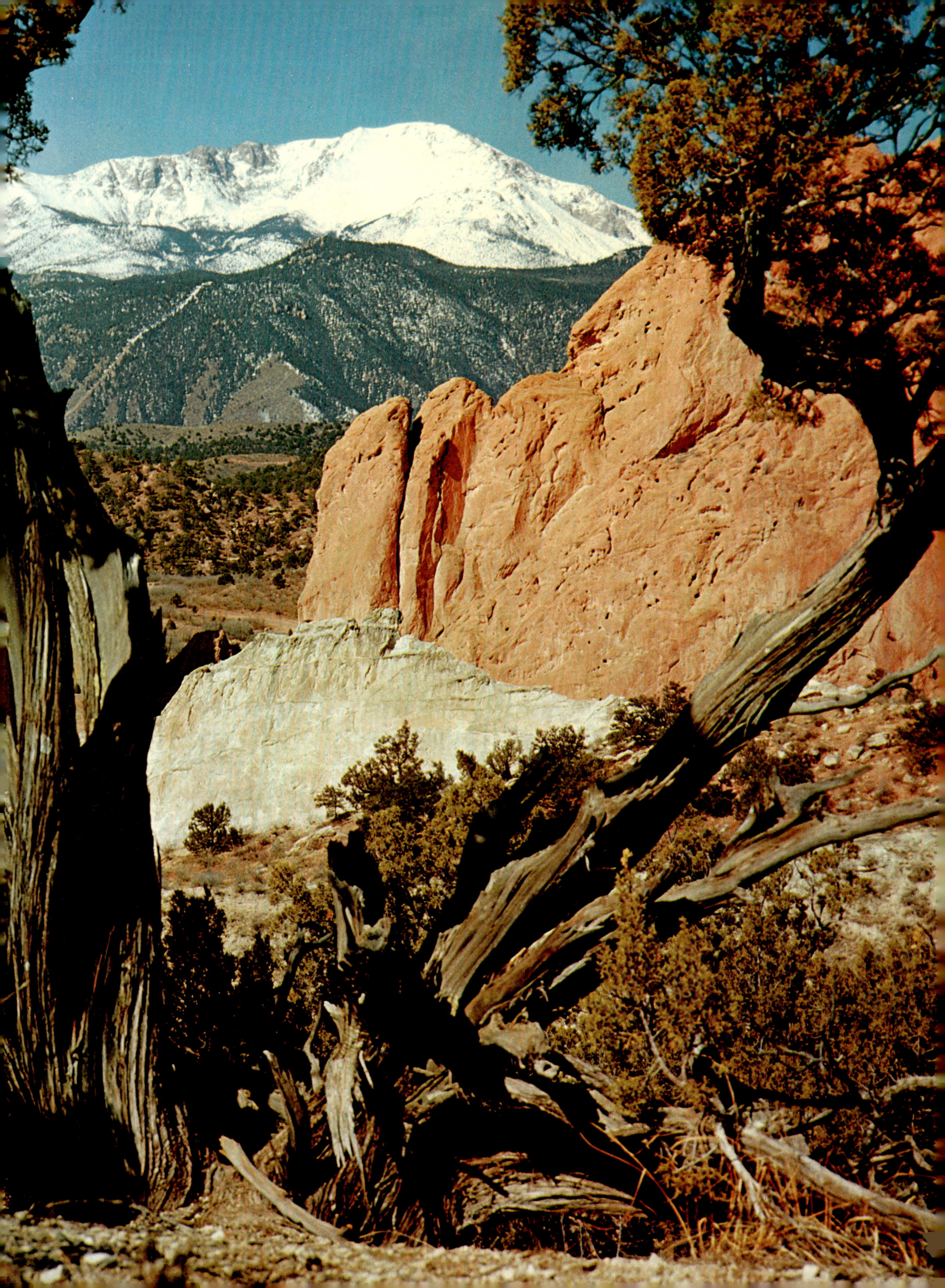

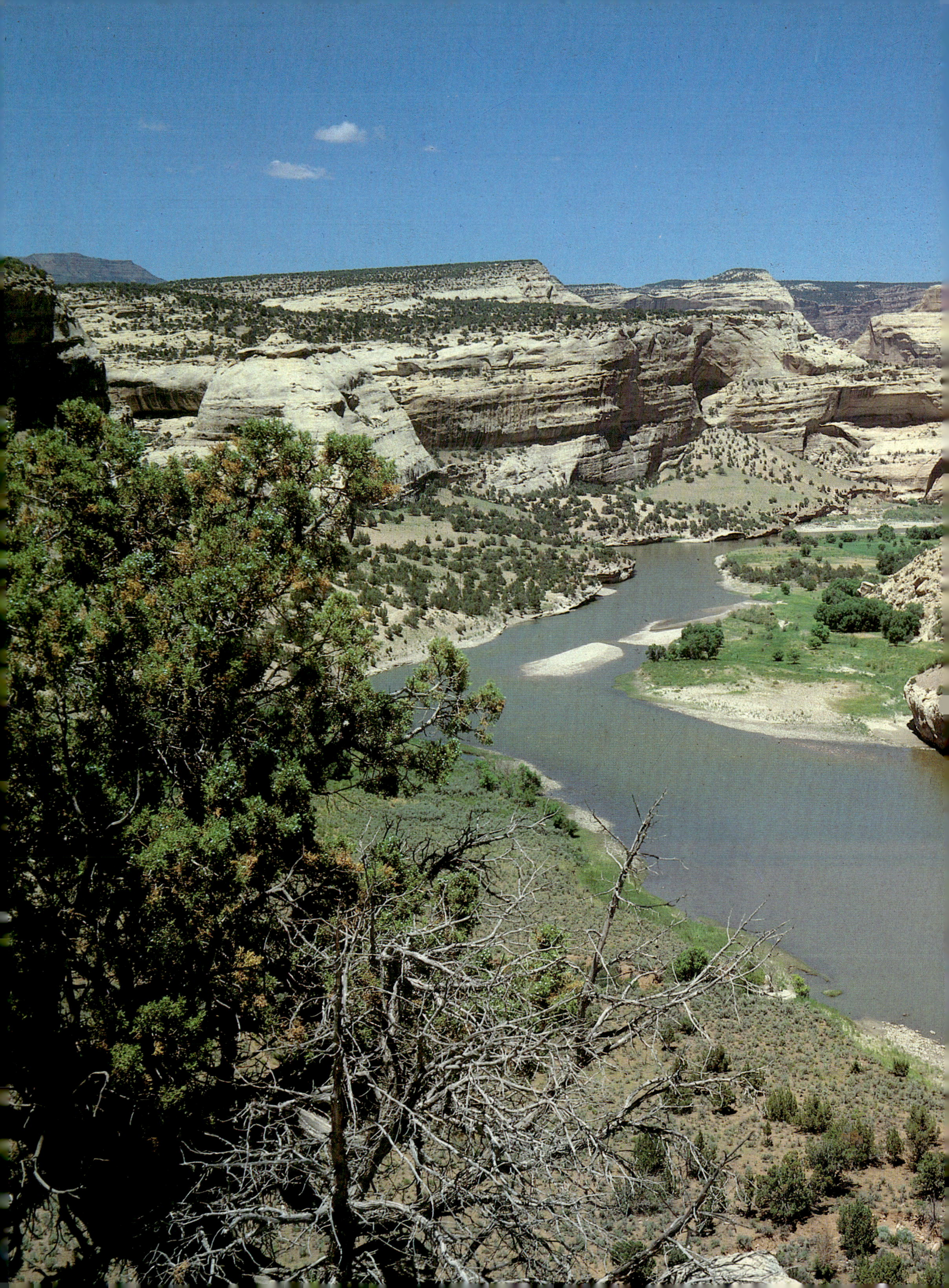

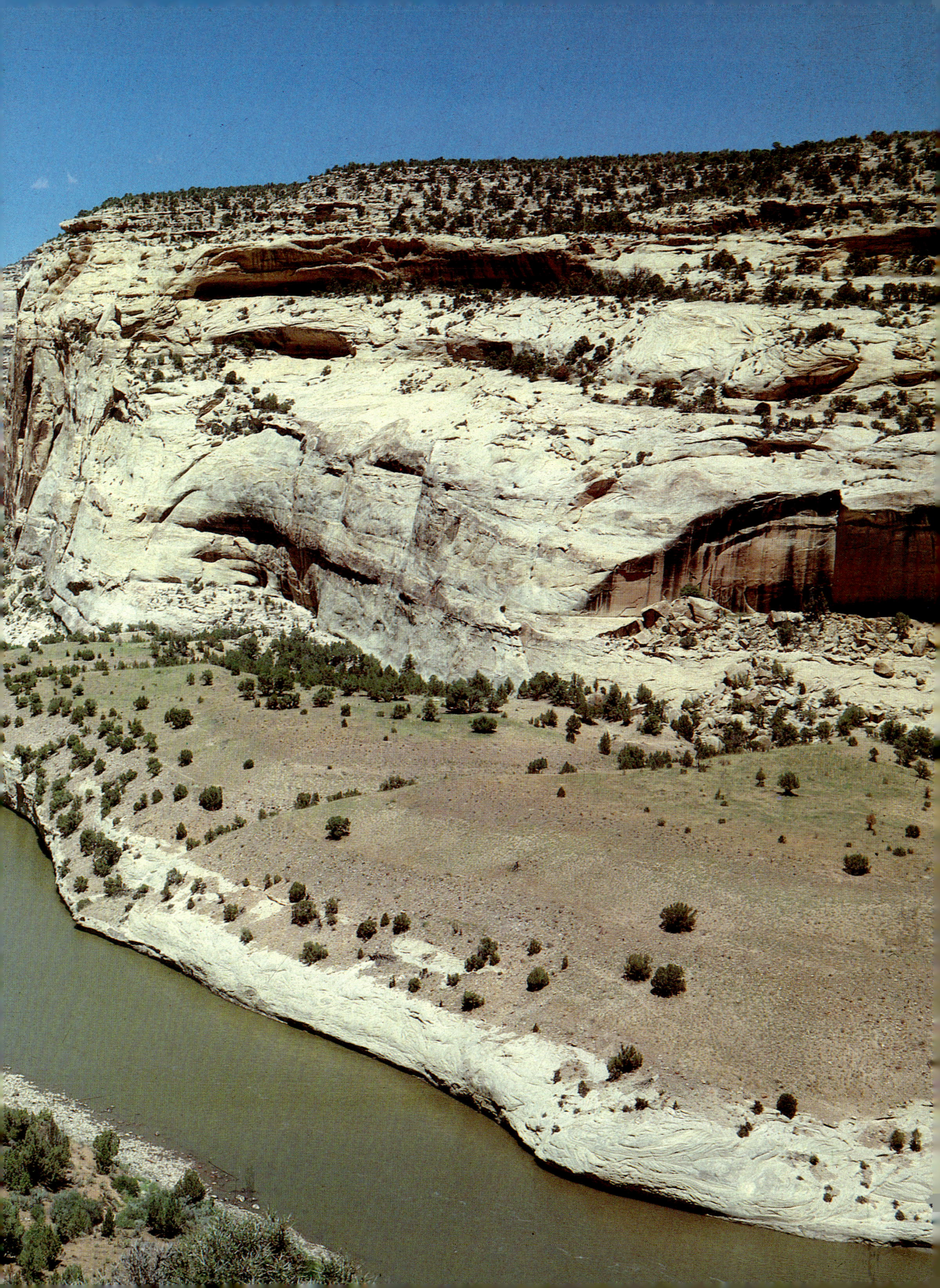

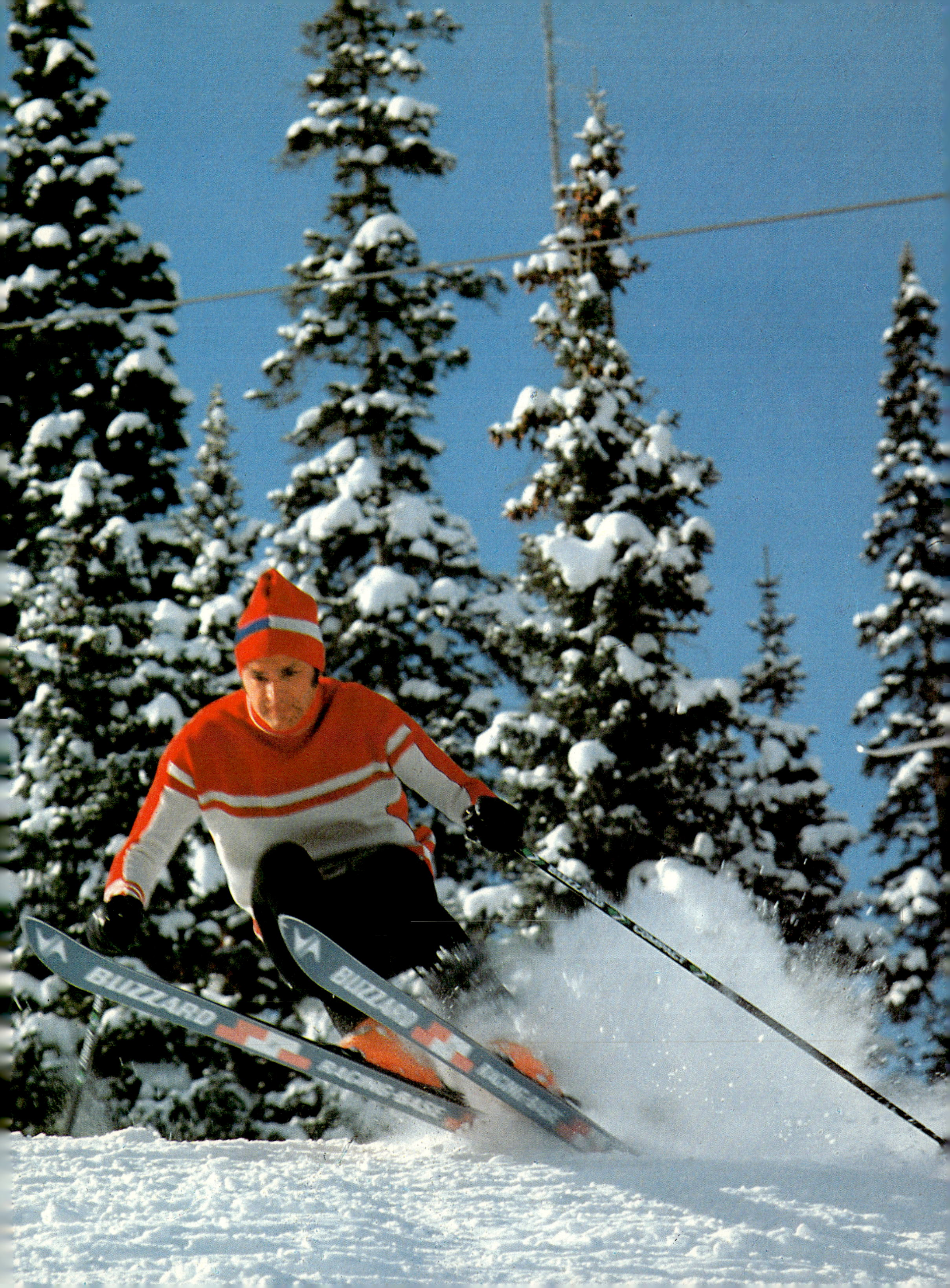
BLIZZARD
BLIZZARD

THINGS TO SEE AND DO

"The scenery bankrupts the English language"
Theodore Roosevelt

During all seasons there are things to see and do in Colorado. In January, there's the National Western Stock Show and Rodeo in Denver. March brings the Western Art Exhibit and free concerts by the Denver Symphony Orchestra. April is the time for the Estes Park Hobby Show and for the Easter Sunrise Services at the Park of the Red Rocks. The Aspen Music Festival, presenting every type of music imaginable, runs practically nonstop through the summer. The Central City Opera offers productions featuring Metropolitan Opera stars during the last two weeks in July. In Fairplay, the last weekend of July, the World's Champion Pack Burro Race is held. August brings in the Shadow Mountain Sailboat Regatta on Grand Lake. A visit to the Denver Botanic Gardens provides a pleasant interlude. In Boulder, one can view the site of the state's first schoolhouse or walk the campus of the University of Colorado. Other sights are Boulder Canyon, Roosevelt National Forest, the World's Largest Open Air Hot Springs Swimming Pool in Glenwood Springs, the Aztec Ruins, and Chaco Canyon. A ride on the old narrow-gauge railroad from Durango to Silverton has an excitement all its own as one looks at many of the state's scenic wonders en route. Fishing and hiking in the San Juan National Forest is always a rewarding experience. And many other special places and events wait to captivate visitors to colorful Colorado.

The state is also known for its industry tours. The Coors Brewery in Golden, Loveland's Great Western Sugar Company, the Climax Molybdenum Company's mining operations in Climax, the Cudahy Packing Company in Brighton, and Pueblo's Colorado Fuel and Iron Company provide a varied intinerary. In Denver, one can visit the Bowman Biscuit Company, the U.S. Mint, Sunstrand Aviation (makers of aerospace power systems), Denver Wholesale Florists, the Packaging Corporation of America, the DENVER POST, the Gates Rubber Company, and the Rio Grande Railway Shops. Of course, Denver is also home to one of the major money-making facilities in the country—the United States Mint, where automatic equipment stamps out half-dollars, quarters, dimes, nickels, and pennies. The building is the largest depository of gold bullion in America outside of Fort Knox, Kentucky—about six billion dollars worth.

Rodeos are held in many towns, but the best known are the Pikes Peak or Bust Rodeo held the second week in August in Colorado Springs, and the Colorado State Fair Rodeo in Pueblo that takes place in late August. In northwest Denver are Elitch Gardens and Lakeside, two fine amusement parks. Elitch offers summer stock theater with Broadway stars; the place is also famous for its exquisite formal flower displays. Lakeside is popular for its stock car races, speedboat rides, and for a toy train that chugs its way all around Lake Rhoda.

The highest highway in the country climbs and twists up 14,260-foot Mount Evans, by Echo Lake and icy Summit Lake, to reach the top of the mountain and give the spectator a truly inspiring view. Laboratories on this summit provide facilities for the study of cosmic rays and other high-altitude phenomena.

Left: Racing excitement is a regularly scheduled event at Purgatory Ski Resort located in the specatular San Juan Mountains, 25 miles north of Durango.

Overleafs: Colorado Ski Country. Symphony on skis.

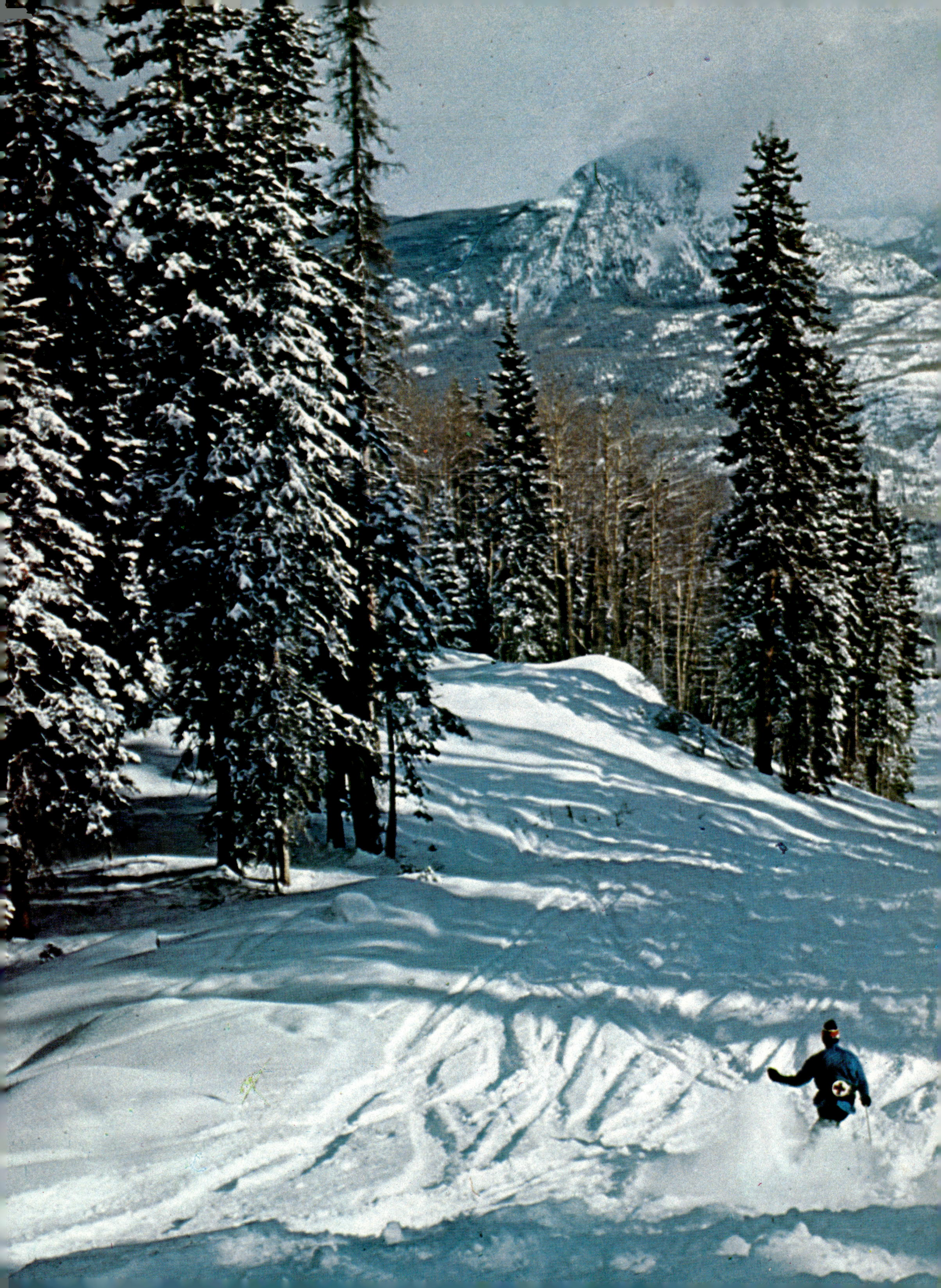

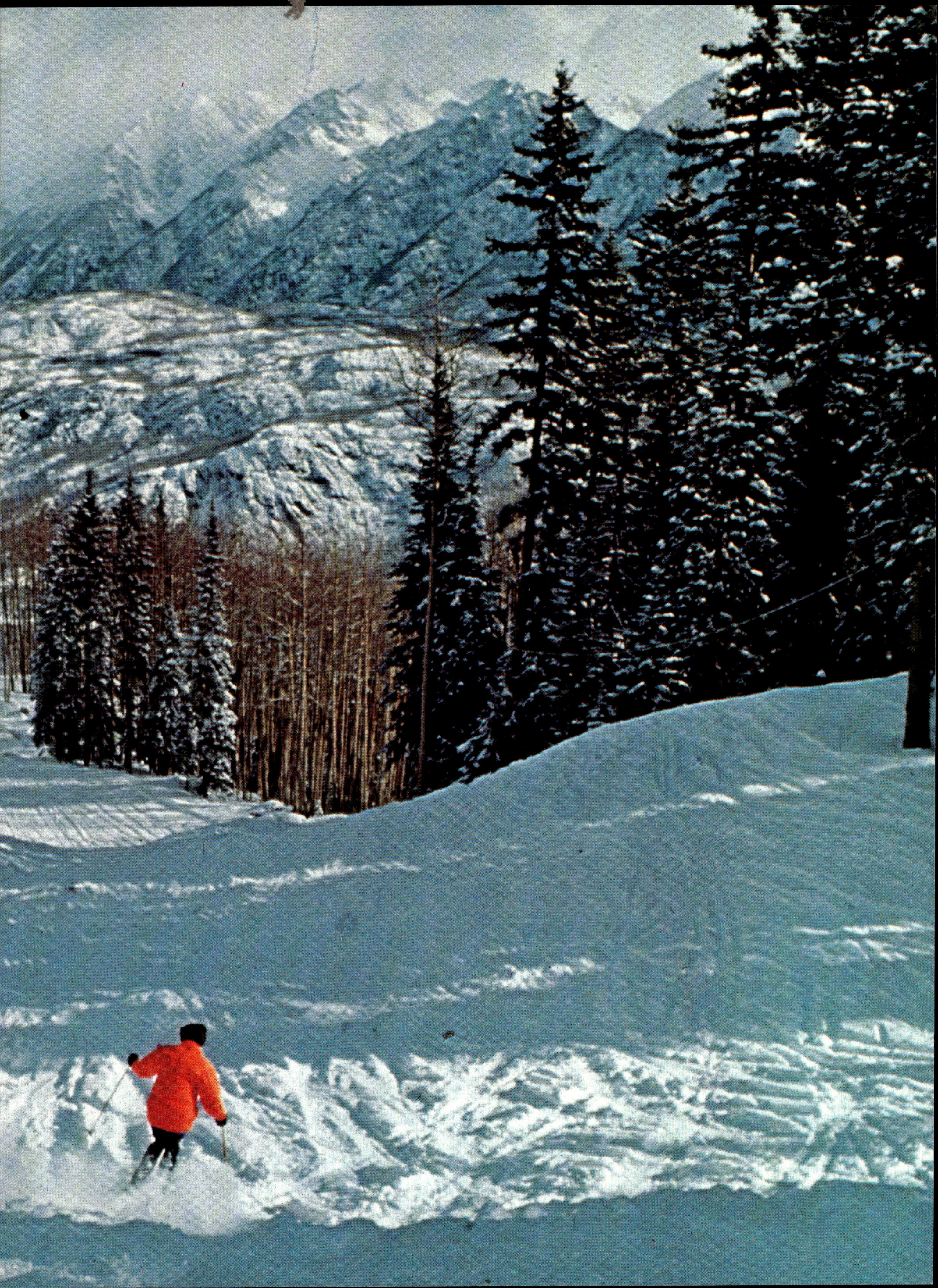

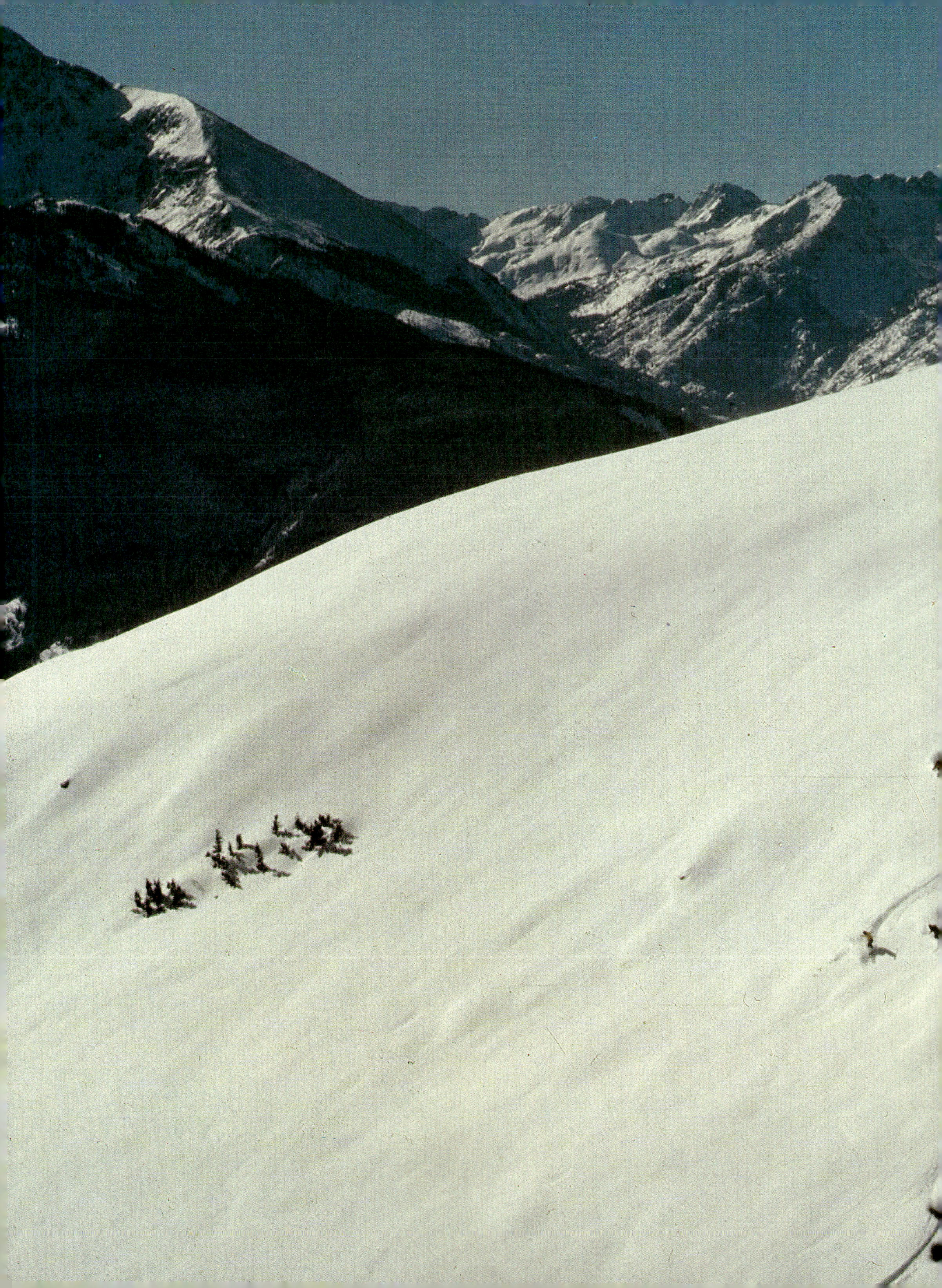

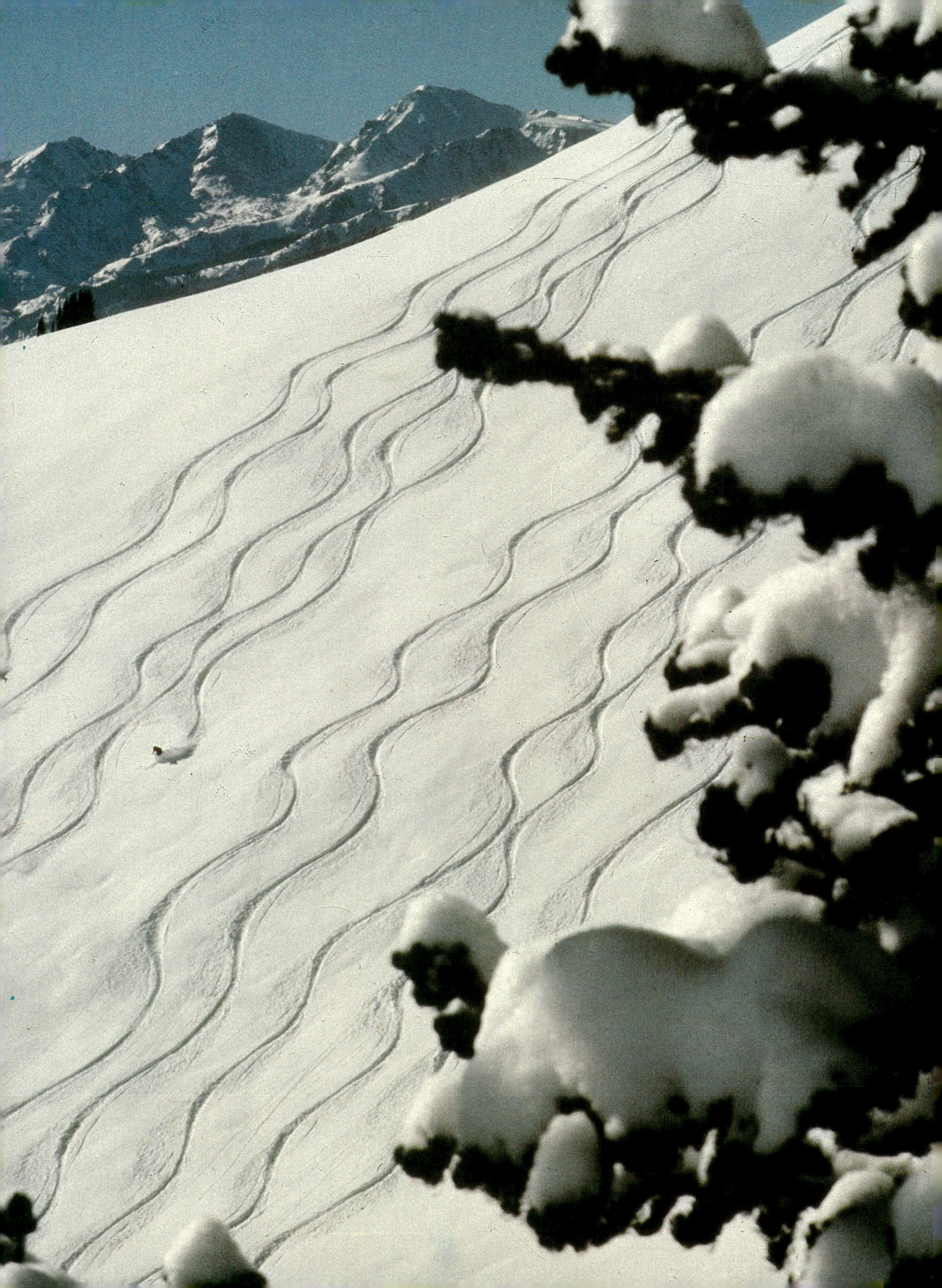

Below:
Monarch Pass, one of the highest in the nation, forms the Continental Divide.

Right:
A luxury year 'round resort south of Purgatory Ski Area.

Left: Taylor Dam and Lake near Gunnison.

Overleaf:
View overlooking beautiful Lake Cristobal located in the heart of the Colorado Rockies.

MONARCH PASS
Elevation 11,312 feet

CONTINENTAL DIVIDE
ATLANTIC   PACIFIC

Theater is alive and well in Colorado. Central City's Annual Summer Festival, Boulder's Shakespeare Festival, the Denver Civic Ballet, the Bonfils Theater, and many other theaters and groups present various offerings of drama and dance throughout the year. The DENVER POST'S "Opera Under the Stars" is an annual presentation of popular musicals or light operas, free to the public. And for a wonderful experience where heroes are rousingly cheered and villains gleefully hissed, many communities present melodramas caricaturing the unique folk lore of the brawling Old West.

Of Denver's numerous museums, most interesting are the Denver Art Museum, the Denver Museum of Natural History in City Park, The Colorado State Historical Museum, the Colorado Railroad Museum, and the Civic Center's Living Arts Center. Outside the state capital, there are the Fine Arts Center at Colorado Springs, and elsewhere in the state the National Carvers Museum, the Pioneer Museum, the Gold Mine Museum showing the H.A.W. Tabor Collection, the Hogans Clock Manor Museum, and the geology museum of the Colorado School of Mines. Of special interest are the Buffalo Bill Museum on Lookout Mountain, the Koshare Indian museum in La Junta, and the El Pueblo Museum featuring a full-scale model of the El Pueblo Fort of 1842. Most of the parks, monuments, recreation areas, and historical sites have their own modest museums focusing on the local scenes.

Another of Colorado's attraction is its mineral springs and spas. Colorado Springs, perhaps the best known of these, is a health and pleasure resort. Manitou Springs is close by. This region also contains the Pikes Peak area, the Garden of the Gods, the Cave of the Winds, Cheyenne Canyon, Seven Falls, and the Will Rogers Shrine of the Sun. Pagosa Springs just west of the Continental Divide, crossed by Wolf Creek Pass, is another popular spa; a 600-foot-long swimming pool is fed year-round by hot and cold sulfur springs. Presidents Teddy Roosevelt and Taft vacationed here. Idaho Springs, Glenwood Springs, Hot Sulphur Springs, and Steamboat Springs all have facilities for enjoying the waters. A beautifully located natural hot springs swimming pool is in the tiny town of Ouray, which is surrounded by 14,000-foot peaks. The changing colors in autumn and the early snow create a breathtaking landscape. Ouray is known as "The Switzerland of America".

The ever-increasing popularity of skiing has meant a real tourist boom for Colorado. The state has more skiing slopes than perhaps any other place in the country, and magnificent slopes they are, too. Vail's reputation was enhanced by former President Ford's preference for the area. Aspen is very likely the most action-packed and bustling ski center in the world, with slopes and conditions to suit every degree of skill. Good skiing is also available in Summit County—a complex of three resorts, Keystone, Copper Mountain, and Breckenridge. Steamboat Village offers skiing for the entire family, from tots to grandparents. The Purgatory Ski Area, northwest of Durango, is the major ski resort in southwestern Colorado.

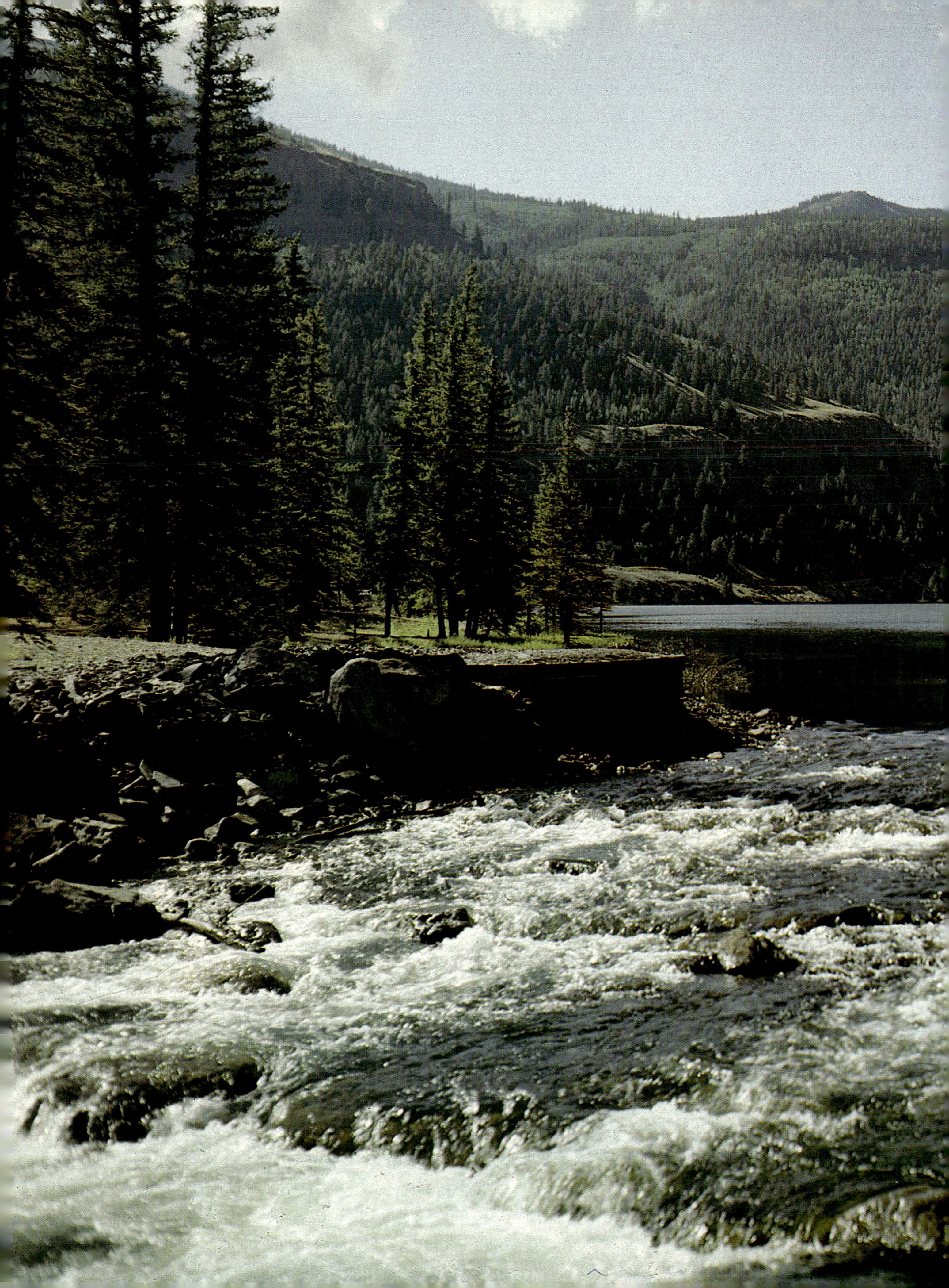

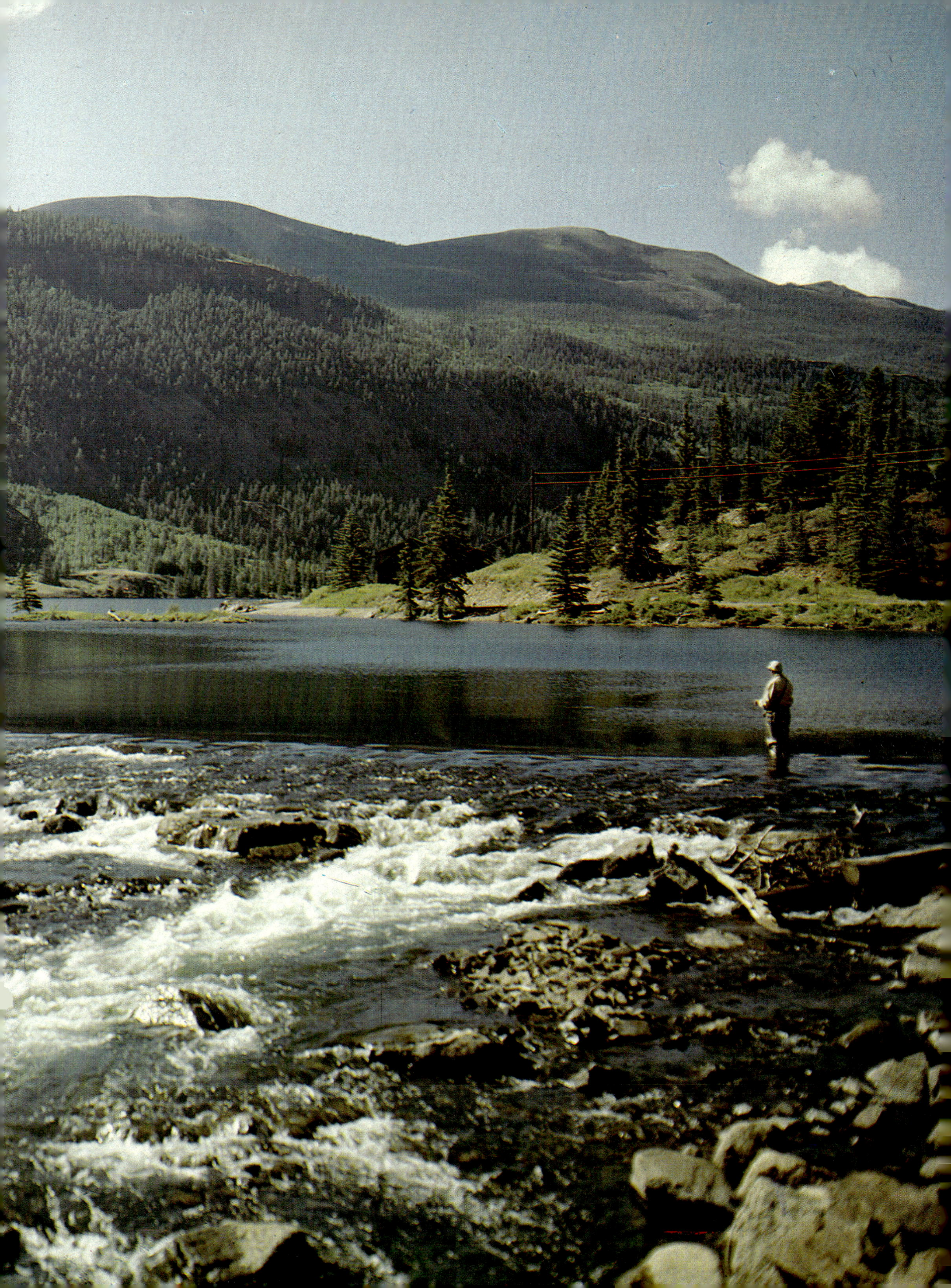

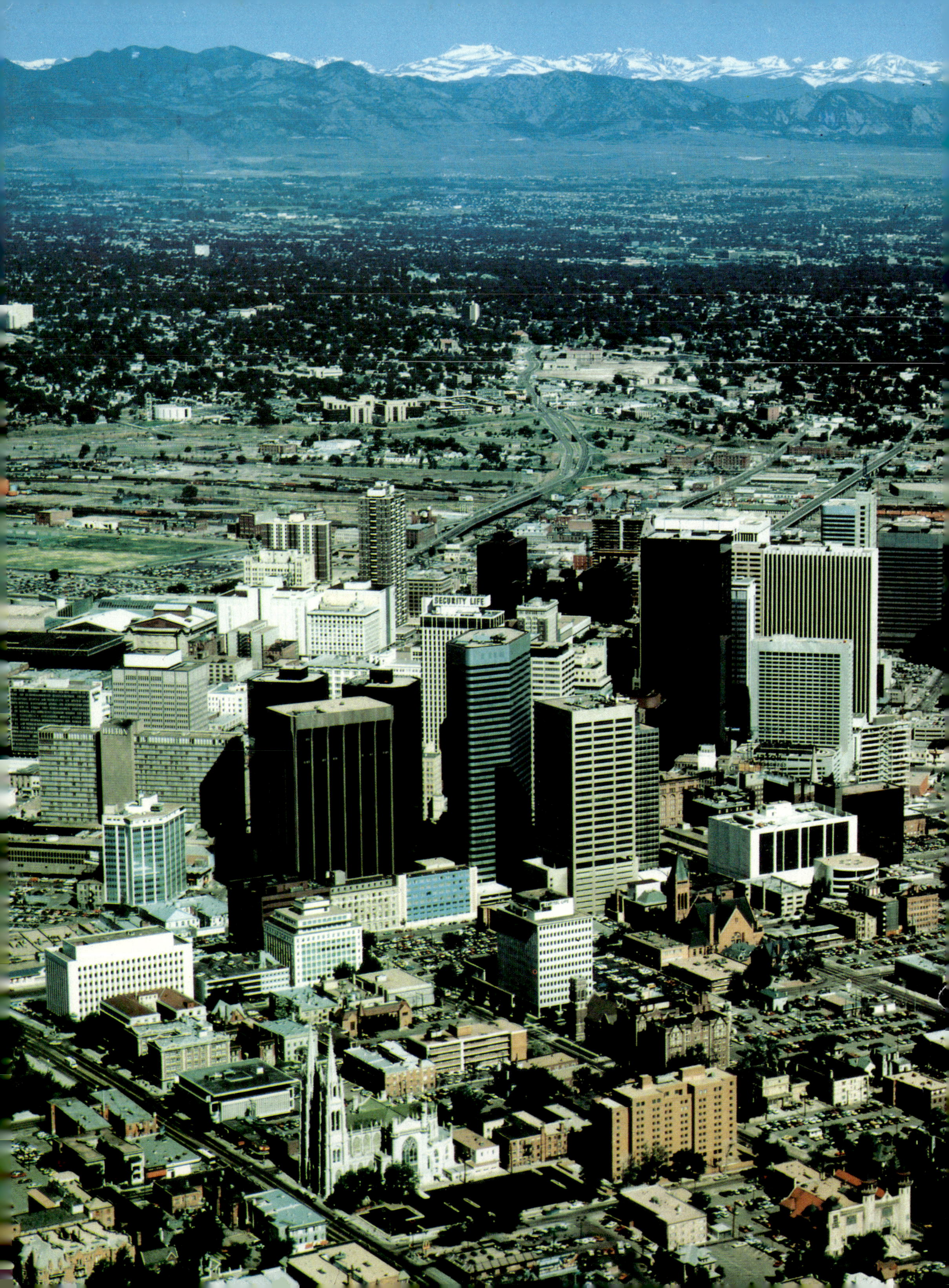
SECURITY LIFE

THE MILE HIGH CITY

*"When I walk down a Denver street,
I always feel as if I were listening
to a brass band."*
Dabney Otis Collins, author (1971)

"Living up in the hills" is how many of Denver's metropolitan residents describe their lifestyle. Sprawled across a plateau a mile above sea level, at the point where the plains of eastern Colorado and the foothills of the Rockies meet, lies Denver, the capital of Colorado, shaded by the titanic, snowcapped peaks that form the Continental Divide. In the city's suburbs, the air is pure and clear, brisk and invigorating. As modern, highrise buildings appear throughout the city in bursts of construction, efforts to retain and restore Denver's Wild West past do not lag far behind.

The city's original tents and cabins were raised on Cherry Creek at what is now Larimer Square in 1858. The present square is a curious blend of recreated shops and cafes that recall the old days rather vividly. But the real cowboys are gone, except for those who come to town for the January National Western Stock Show and Rodeo.

The State Capitol rotunda offers the best overall view of the city. The fantastic Rocky Mountains rise on the west, while to the east stretch the sweeping Great Plains; Denver itself is spread out below. On the thirteenth step of the State Capitol is a sign pointing out that this point is exactly one mile above sea level. Well...actually there's another marker three steps above this one because students from Colorado State's engineering school discovered the original marker was in error.

The rotunda bears a striking resemblance to the dome of the nation's capitol building. Denver is, in fact, so similar to Washington, D.C. that it has acquired the nickname "Little Washington". Colorado's State Capitol dome is coated with $110,000 worth of Colorado gold leaf. The wainscoting throughout the Capitol is of priceless Colorado rose onyx. Onyx of this color comes from Beulah, Colorado, and has never been found anywhere else in the world. The marble used to construct the floors and the impressive staircase came from Marble, Colorado. The largest single block of marble ever quarried (weighing 100 tons), also came from the town of Marble and now marks the tomb of the Unknown Soldier in Arlington Cemetery.

Denver's City Park is a 640-acre tract with two lakes and spreading green lawns. The Museum of Natural History, with its Habitat Zoo, is situated in the park.

The entire Civic Center complex, located in the heart of the city, is excellently designed. The idea for the Center originated with Mayor Robert Spear in 1904. He planned the project to resemble the State Capitol building, but work wasn't begun until 1919. The complex was finally completed in 1932.

One especially noteworthy attraction of the many that Denver offers is Molly Brown's House at 1340 Pennsylvania Street. The story goes that when Molly and her gold-miner husband Johnny Brown moved into their Capitol Hill mansion they were snubbed by Denver's society as being merely NOUVEAU RICHE. Ironically enough, it is Molly Brown's House that is visited more often than any of the other fine mansions. Molly was an intelligent woman not easily intimidated, and she won a place in Colorado's history by an act of heroism that took place on the high seas. She was aboard the TITANIC on its fateful voyage, and when the ship was sinking, she took charge of a lifeboat, and refusing to give up she ordered the oar crew to row while she spread her chinchilla cape over a group of children to keep them warm. Ever after she was known as the "unsinkable Molly Brown".

Left and Overleaf: Downtown Denver.

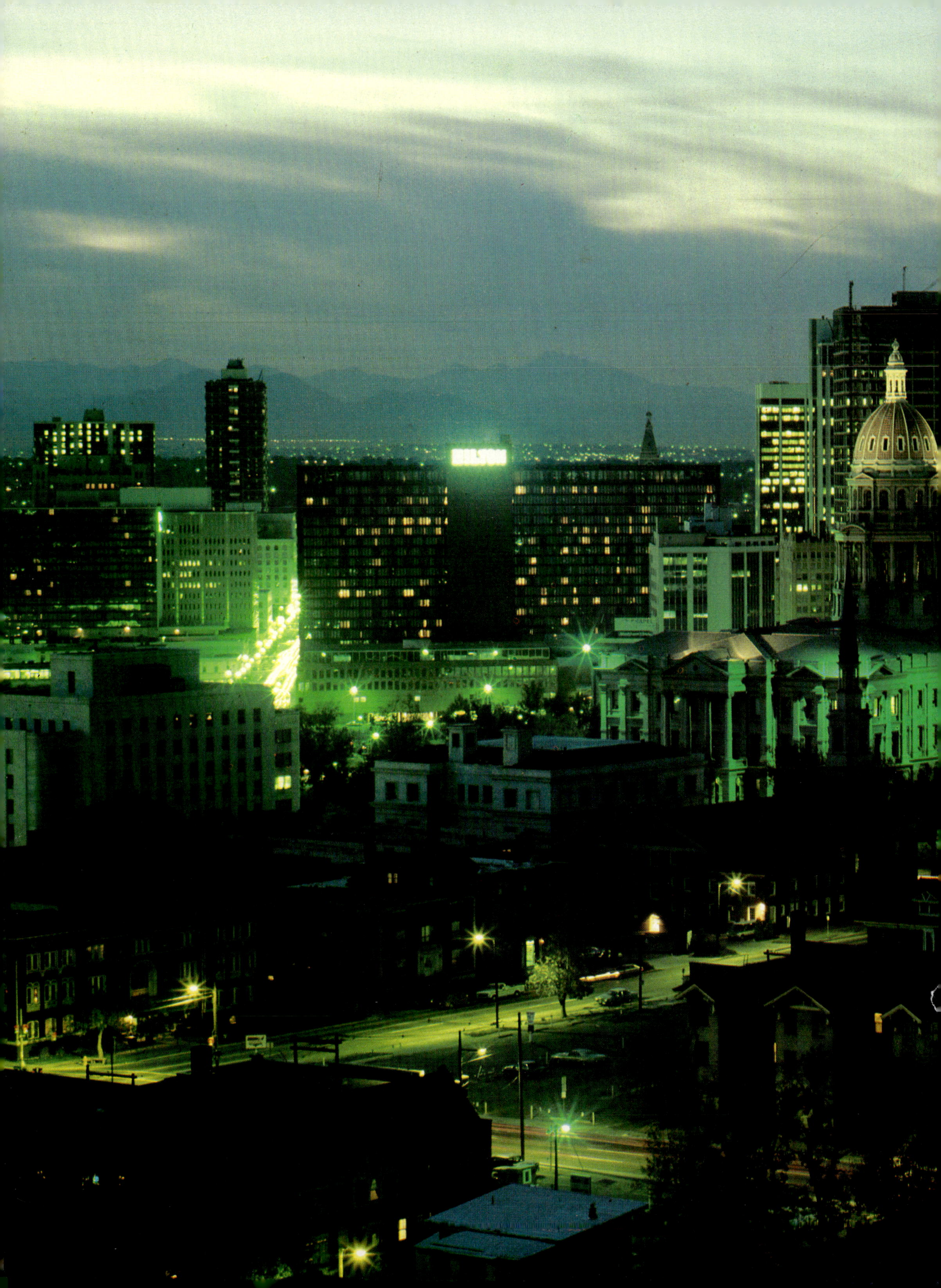

Upper left:
Red Rocks Amphitheatre.

Far left:
Botanic Gardens, an extraordinary complex that includes the Boettcher Memorial Conservatory and York Street Gardens.

Above: Denver Mile High Stadium.

Left: "Unsinkable" Molly Brown Home, 1340 Pennsylvania St.

Overleaf: The beautifully delicate Columbine is the State flower of Colorado.